Rhode Island ADVENTURE DIVING II

Marlene & Don Snyder,
Editing Authors

George Flynn * Cover Photographer
David Snyder * Technical Assistant
Marlene Snyder * Graphic Designer

Disclaimer

The authors of *Rhode Island Adventure Diving II* have made every effort to assure the accuracy of the contents of this book. However, no warranty or guarantee is expressed or implied that the information contained in *Rhode Island Adventure Diving II* is accurate or correct, or may not contain errors. The authors shall in no way be responsible for any consequential, incidental or exemplary loss or damage resulting from the use of any of the graphics or printed information contained in *Rhode Island Adventure Diving II*. The authors disclaim any liability for omissions, errors, alterations and misprints and hereby give notice that *Rhode Island Adventure Diving II* is not to be used for navigation.

> Historic shipwrecks are the property of the State of Rhode Island, nothing may be removed. Rhode Island Antiquities Act (G.L, Chp., 43.45.1)
>
> Please read the "Preserving Shipwrecks" article in this book.

© **1995 by Marlene & Don Snyder**
199 Steiger Drive, Westfield, Massachusetts 01085
Telephone (413) 568-1083

First Printing, April 1995

ISBN 0-9645288-1-9

Dedication

With love and affection to our family and friends who make life an adventure

Acknowledgements

The contributions and cooperation of the following individuals and organizations made this book possible:

Robert Bachand

Philip Budlong

William Campbell

Bob Clarke, Sr.

Philip Coburn

Tim Coleman

LeRoy Cook

John Donovan

Ed Hamilton

John Jagschitz

Jamestown Library

Jamestown Museum

Jamestown Press

Jim Jenney

Henry Keatts

Bertram Lippincott III

Sue Maden

John McAniff

Vincent Neri

Newport Historical Society

Newport Public Library

Andrew Nota

Jim Pemantell

Providence Journal

Susan Ryan

Save The Bay

Walter Schroder

Larry Silvia

Brian Skerry

David Snyder

Mark Snyder

Melissa Snyder created the drawings on this page when she was very young

Charley Soares

Kenneth Stromgren

Margaret Stromgren

David Swain

Charlotte Taylor

Lynne Tungett

University of Rhode Island

Rick Walker

Lawrence Webster

Edward Welch

Westfield Athenaeum

DeDe Snyder—With special thanks

Table Of Contents
& Dive Site Locations

Bonnett Point 6

Jones Ledge 6

Whale Rock 6

Narragansett ✛ Narrow River 6

✛ Barge 6 & 50

Point Judith

Charlestown

Misquamicut

Watch Hill

Samson 58

Skyraider 60
Hellcat 26 & 28

Napatree Point 48 & Watch Hill Reefs 48

Hercules 30
Unknown 66
Metis 42
Lake Crystal 38

Mary Arnold 40
Progress 40
Heroine 32
Annapolis 2

N

Spartan 62

Block Island

Idene 34

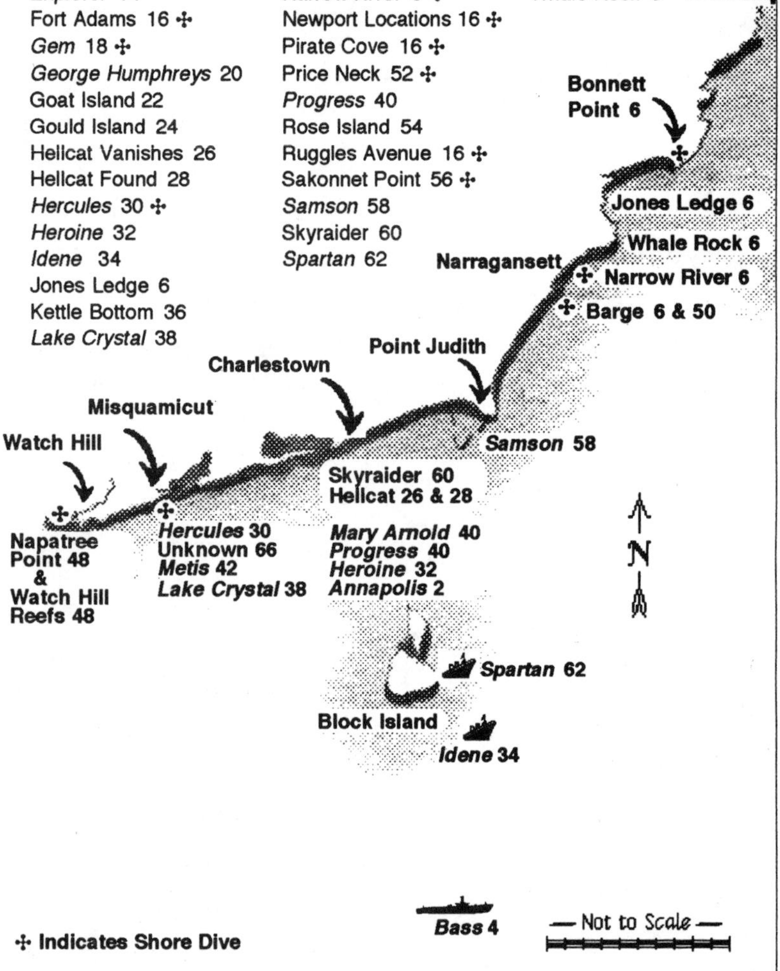

✛ Indicates Shore Dive

Bass 4

— Not to Scale —

iii

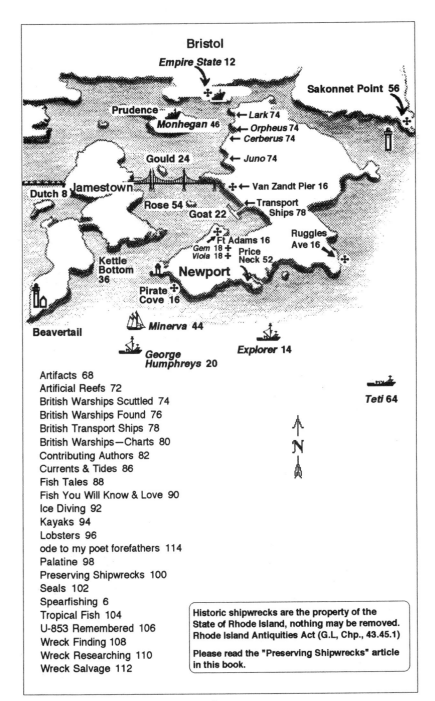

Bristol

Empire State 12

Sakonnet Point 56

Prudence

Monhegan 46

← *Lark* 74
← *Orpheus* 74
← *Cerberus* 74

Gould 24

← *Juno* 74

Dutch 8

Jamestown

Rose 54

Goat 22

✝← Van Zandt Pier 16

←Transport
Ships 78

Ruggles
Ave 16

Ft Adams 16
Gem 18 ✝
Viola 18 ✝

Price
Neck 52

Kettle
Bottom
36

Newport

Pirate ✝
Cove 16

Beavertail

Minerva 44

*George
Humphreys* 20

Explorer 14

Teti 64

N

Historic shipwrecks are the property of the
State of Rhode Island, nothing may be removed.
Rhode Island Antiquities Act (G.L, Chp., 43.45.1)

Please read the "Preserving Shipwrecks" article
in this book.

Beneath The Shimmering Sea

by Marlene & Don Snyder

In The Beginning
25,000 years ago, a sheet of glacial ice 400 feet thick—higher than the Newport Bridge—engulfed Rhode Island as far south as Block Island in a cryogenic sleep.

Over the next nineteen thousand years, the sun's warmth caused the ice sheet to recede, exposing the colossal valley system that the glacier had gouged across Rhode Island.

Magnificent Shoreline
As the ocean swelled with billions of gallons of glacial water, it swept over its shore, then located 70 miles beyond Block Island, and began a centuries-long inland advance, finally drowning the valleys 5,000 years ago creating Rhode Island's four hundred miles of magnificent scenic shoreline.

Transformed from a frigid wasteland to a wonderland, with midbay temperatures of 68° Fahrenheit during the balmy summers, and 32° Fahrenheit in the moderate winters, the Rhode Island coastline and Narragansett Bay became one of the most provocative and fascinating places on earth.

The Bay Is Immense
Rhode Island's Narragansett Bay is immense: 25 miles long and 10 miles wide, with an average depth of 26 feet and a maximum depth of 184 feet off Newport's Castle Hill. The bay's 132 square miles of water cover ten percent of Rhode Island.

The bay is scientifically classified as an *estuary* created by freshwater run-off and rivers that flow into and mix with its

v

seawater. It is a relatively small estuary. By contrast, Chesapeake Bay, the largest estuary in the United States, is 30 times larger. Most of the life in the bay is dependent on nourishment from organic material produced when microscopic, one-celled, floating plants called *phytoplankton*, trap solar energy and, by photosynthesis, convert that energy into food for themselves.

Nutritionally Rich

Because the bay is a nutritionally rich 706 billion gallon estuary, it is a nursery and hunting ground for hundreds of species of native marine life as well as for transient marine life from many of the world's seas.

Wonders Below

To venture below the shimmering surface of Rhode Island's waters is to enter a hidden realm that is one of the most mysterious, intriguing, dangerous, and, consequently, exciting places on earth.

Twenty or more feet of subsea visibility is common at many of Rhode Island's shore and offshore dive sites.

Name your snorkeling or diving interests—obsessions!—wreck diving, tropical fish collecting, photography, just observing: they can be satisfied in Rhode Island waters.

The original *Rhode Island Adventure Diving* book and this volume, Rhode *Island Adventure Diving II,* describe nearly one hundred fascinating and exciting onshore and offshore diving locations carefully selected to satisfy the desires of the most discriminating divers.

We Must Not Fail Her

Rhode Island waters and their marine life were once nearly destroyed by the very people who loved them so much.

In 1793, America's Industrial Revolution began when a Rhode Island textile mill on the Blackstone River went into operation and Narragansett Bay became a receptacle for industrial and municipal waste.

The worst era was during World War II and the post-war years, 1940-50. Thanks to the efforts of many state and federal agencies and public and private organizations, Rhode Island waters are being restored.

Beginning as a frozen wasteland 25,000 years ago, Rhode Island and her ocean continue to fulfill their destiny as one of the greatest wonders of the planet.

The future of Rhode Island's ocean is in our hands. We must not fail her.

Barge & U.S. Submarine Collide

by Marlene & Don Snyder
with John Warszawski

- *Annapolis*
- Wooden Barge

- Chart # 13215
- Charlestown
  Breachway
  3.5 NM South
- 14535.4
  43945.9
- Depth 120 feet

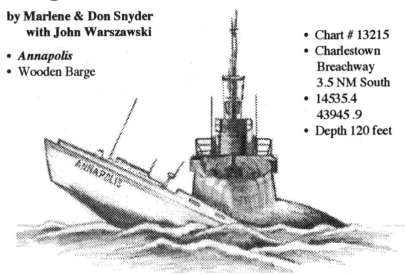

Providence Journal

Saturday, February 18, 1945

SUBMARINE, BARGE COLLIDE OFF COAST

Latter Sinks But No One Is Hurt
in Accident Off Charlestown

Following a collision with a U.S. submarine, a wooden barge sank off Charlestown shortly after midnight Friday night, but there were no injuries to personnel aboard either the underseas craft or the barge, the navy reported last night.

The barge, the *Annapolis*, 229 feet long with a 40-foot beam, was owned by the Peter Dougherty Company of Baltimore and had a cargo of 2200 tons of coal. Harrison Company, Boston was the barge agent.

Capt. Bennis Cidale, of the *Carroll and Bennis*, A Stonnington dragger, last night brought a rowboat, a liferaft and two life preservers from the sunken barge. They were found floating several miles off Block Island.

Captain Cidale reported a large area of water covered with debris from the barge, and part of the wreckage also drifted into Block Island.

Breach Of Security

It would have been a breach of security if the accompanying newspaper account had divulged the name of the U.S. submarine. World War II was still in progress.

Diving The *Annapolis*

Wreck diver John Warszawski, of Jamestown, Rhode Island, provided the following description of the remains of the *Annapolis*.

The 228-foot-long wreck has collapsed over the years and is now broken up and scattered over a large debris field. The bow, which once rose 25 feet off the bottom, has now collapsed and is no more than 10-15 feet in height.

The most recognizable feature of the wreck is a section of an engine or boiler which rises vertically 5-6 feet off the bottom. It was common for manned barges to have engines and boilers to gen-

erate heat and power.

Protruding 2-3 feet above the ocean floor is a section of the hull, nearly 80 feet long, which curves eerily into the cloudy distance. Posts rise like tombstones along the top of the deteriorating hull, a grim reminder that a once proud ship died at this location.

The coal piled in and around the wreck sparkles like black diamonds when hit with a diver's light, hence the alternate name of this wreck, *Black Diamond*.

The extensive remains of another wooden vessel are mingled with the wreckage of the *Annapolis*.

The *Amelia Pereira*?

Some divers have speculated that the remains of the other vessel mingled with the Annapolis are those of the Amelia Pereira.

She was an 88-foot-long, wooden fishing schooner, built at the John James Shipyard, Essex, Massachusetts.

The *Amelia Pereira* is reported to have sunk before World War II at approximately this same location.

Charlestown Beach

Charlestown Breachway

Annapolis

3

U.S. Navy Sinks One Of Its Own

by Marlene & Don Snyder
with Capt. Bill Palmer

- *Bass* (SS-164)
- U.S. submarine
  341.5 feet long
  27.6 foot beam
  2,620 surface tons
  Steel hull

- Block Island
  8.2 NM south
  Chart # 13205
  14560.8
  43817.4

Scuba Diver Finds *Bass*

In 1965 a fishing boat skipper located an unidentified submarine with his electronic bottom scanner. A scuba diving team headed by Michael DeCamp explored the submarine, which was identified by a submarine history buff, Joseph A. Palmer, no relation to Captain Bill Palmer, as the *Bass*.

U.S. Submarine *Bass*

Built at the Portsmouth, New Hampshire Naval Shipyard in 1924, the *Bass* had a crew of 80 officers and seamen. Designed as a combat submarine, she was converted to a merchant submarine in the 1940s to carry cargo and military troops. Her gigantic proportions—length 341.5 feet, weight 2,620 tons— were not equaled until the atomic submarine *Nautilus* was launched in 1955.

Although they had an operating range of 12,000 miles, these merchant submarines were never successfully deployed.

Their leviathan hulk caused their screws to come out of the water when they dove. Submerged they were almost impossible to maneuver.

Their powerful diesel-electric propulsion engines were defective. And, worst of all, the *Bass* leaked! Not a great vessel. In 1942, a fire in the *Bass's* aft battery room asphyxiated 25 of the 80 man crew.

Stripped By The Navy

Stripped by the Navy and used as a target vessel, the *Bass* was sunk by an Anti-Submarine

4

PBY-5A aircraft with a depth charge in March 1945.

Diving The *Bass*

Only the most accomplished and experienced deep wreck divers should dive the *Bass*.

What you see is a magnificent sight—a completely intact submarine sitting upright in 160 feet of water.

The *Bass* sank bow first and broke clean at a forward bulkhead. The two portions are 50-75 feet from each other at right angles.

The all bronze conning tower is in great shape. It is virtually impossible to enter it through the tiny outside hatch while wearing scuba gear.

Entry to the main hull is through a small hatch halfway down the face of the severed bulkhead. The hatchway opens into the engine room. The engine was blown off its mounts and the room is filled with cables, conduit, and piping.

To reach the control room one hundred feet distant, the diver must first swim along the port wall of the engine room, carefully avoiding the piles of debris, go through a bulkhead, and swim the length of the galley.

Ladders lead from the control room up into the conning tower. It is not advisable to do much in the conning tower because of the silt.

Use of a wreck reel is essential. It is very easy to become disoriented on the *Bass*, particularly when the disturbed sediment reduces visibility to zero.

The severed bow portion contained the officers lounge and the forward torpedo room. It is wide open like a tube. Divers can swim to the closed torpedo room hatch.

Bill Palmer Was there First

During a dive on the *Bass* in 1989, Captain Bill Palmer found the submarine's spare helm hidden behind a couch in the officers' lounge. Someone apparently hid it there before the *Bass* was sunk, planning to come back after the sinking and retrieve it as a unique souvenir. Forty-five years later, Bill was there first.

5

Narragansett Shore Spearfishing

by Marlene & Don Snyder

West Passage—Bonnett Point To Narragansett
- Chart # 13223
    1. **Bonnet Point**—41° 28' 10" N & 71° 25' 20" W
    2. **Jones Ledge**—.45 NM southwest of Bonnet Point
    3. **Whale Rock**—1.5 NM southwest of Bonnet Point
    4. **Narrow River Clumps**—2 NM southwest of Bonnet Point
    5. **Narragansett Barge**—.5 NM west of Clump Rocks

Extraordinary Spearfishing
The 2-nautical-mile area from Bonnet Point southwest to the Clumps at the mouth of the Narrow River offers some of the finest spearfishing in Narragansett Bay—when the conditions are right.

With the possible exception of Clump Rocks and Bonnet Point, these five sites are only accessible by boat. Diving can be hazardous to your health and to your boat unless you take every precaution.

All five locations are at the mouth of the West Passage and all face to the southeast and the open ocean, making them particularly vulnerable to wind and wave action. The current at both ebb and flood tides, especially spring and moon tides, can be unmanageable. The Narrow River flows in at the Clumps adding to the hazard at that location.

Dive only at slack tide when there is no surge. Listen to a current weather report and use your tide table to calculate a window of opportunity. There is always another day, but only if you are careful.

1. Bonnet Point
Bonnet Point offers ideal conditions for spearfishing. A reef begins at the point and extends north along the shoreline for nearly a mile. The reef breaks the surface at intervals and drops to 25-foot-depths as it extends in a series of rocky caverns, overhangs, peaks, and valleys several hundred feet from the shore line to the sandy bottom. Huge tautog come in on

the tide to feed on the mussels that cling to the rocky shoreline.

2. Jones Ledge
Jones Ledge is extraordinary. The ledge is an undersea wonderland characterized by peaks and valleys that extend from just under the surface to dark mysterious pools 30 to 40 feet below. The subsurface pools are often churning with tautog of awesome proportions whose tameness indicates that they rarely encounter humans.

Jones Ledge has claimed ships in the past. It appears to be an ideal location for wreck finding.

3. Whale Rock
Whale rock is a pinnacle that rises fifty feet from the ocean floor to form a half acre granite island. Its sides are littered with huge boulders and the cast-iron remains of the destroyed lighthouse. You can hide in the boulders and, when they are in, have your pick of some of the biggest tautog and stripers that you will ever see.

4. Clump Rocks & Boat Ramp
Clump Rocks are located 300-400 yards southeast of the mouth of the Narrow River. Depths around the rocks average 10-15 feet.

Just west of the Route 1A bridge, on the south side of the Narrow River inlet is a public access from Starr Drive and a boat ramp, in poor condition.

Spearfishing on the outer edges can be excellent. Although it is possible to venture up the Narrow River on a rising tide, boats and currents make it hazardous.

5. Narragansett Barge
Approximately .5 NM west of Clump Rocks is the wreck of an automobile barge just off the Narragansett Beach.

The barge is an excellent spearfishing location described elsewhere in this book.

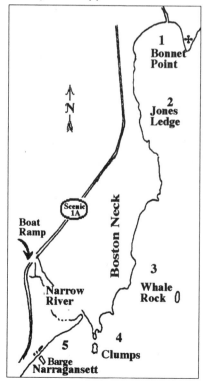

7

Dutch Island Treasure

by Marlene & Don Snyder

- **Dutch Island**
- Jamestown
- Chart #13223

Dutch Island Lighthouse

Dutch Island Overview

Dutch Island sits like a wedge in the West Passage, approximately 600 yards north, across Dutch Harbor, from Jamestown's Fort Getty public camping area.

Artifacts

Dutch Island was inhabited by Indians for 4,500 years, and was a trading post and military stronghold for over 350 years.

It doesn't take much imagination to visualize the treasures in the waters surrounding Dutch Island.

Shipwrecks, antique bottles, clay pipes, pottery, silverware, crockery, china, military insignia, military belt buckles, metal statues, and the like are there to be observed.

Fascinating And Deadly

The abandoned Dutch Island Lighthouse is located at the southwestern tip of Dutch Island.

Extending from the shoreline at the base of the lighthouse for 100 yards toward the lighted gong buoy is a fascinating and dangerous reef.

The long, narrow, knife-like reef drops gradually from the shore to nearly 60 feet below the surface at its terminus, half way to the buoy.

Come to the reef very cautiously, at slack tide. Jagged portions of the reef lie just below the surface of the water.

Anchor carefully as the current changes from ebb to flow here very quickly.

Teeming With Native Fish

When they are running, the reef is often swarming with legal size tautog and stripers. They can be pursued with camera or spear gun. It is a natural habitat, teeming with native fish of all sizes. The steep, picturesque walls of the reef, alive with marinelife of every variety is a thrilling sight.

Ominous Shape

About halfway between the shore and the end of the reef, in 30 feet of water there is a fascinating structure. You may see the huge chain links first, draped like a sea serpent over the top of the reef, 5 feet below the surface. The chain snakes 20 feet down the steep western side of the reef to the ocean floor.

Suddenly an ominous shape looms upward. At least 6 feet square at the base, it rises 12-15 feet toward the surface. The remains of a ship? No. A sunken gong buoy, its erector-set metal structure still in good repair, abandoned and forgotten here for some unknown reason in the dim past. That sight alone is worth the trip.

A History Of Shipwrecks

Coast Guard Wreck Reports from the past and more recent NOOA Reports describe ships of every variety that have sunk in Dutch Island waters.

Sloop *Two-Catherines* Sinks

The September 8, 1821 edition of the *Newport Mercury* reported that the 100-foot-long, 3 masted sloop *Two-Catherines* of Providence had sunk in a gale after striking a rock at the south end of Dutch Island. The officers and crew were saved, but the ship and cargo, 16,000 bushels of salt, were a total loss.

On a recent scuba diving excursion to this same location, a seven-inch-long, hand forged, brass spike, protruding from a one-quarter-inch-thick, seven-inch-long "T" shaped piece of brass strapping was found. From the *Two-Catherines*? Research will tell.

The figure-head of a woman has not been found. Yet!

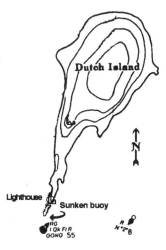

East Passage Barge Wrecks

by John Stanford

Graphic by
Albert Langner
& Marlene Snyder

Transportation Life-Line

Newport Harbor and the East Passage of Narragansett Bay have been the transportation life-line of Rhode Island for three centuries.

Rose Island and Goat Island which lie in the outer harbor form an informal boundary between the harbor and the deep waters of the East Passage.

Vessels of Every Description

Vessels of every description ply their trade on this marine highway.

On any given day a careful observer may spot one of the most common commercial vessels seen on the bay: a tug and barge combination. The barges are used to haul varied cargoes, including fuel, coal, gravel and the like.

Sometime In The Past

Sometime in the past, one of those barges never made it to its destination. The unidentified barge went down in 55 feet of water, precisely in the middle of the waterway midway between Goat Island and Rose Island.

A Mystery

The approximately 100-foot-long, upside-down wooden barge rises approximately 15 feet off the bottom at its highest point. When it sank is a complete mystery.

There is a second smaller barge, approximately 50 feet in length, just to the north of the first barge.

Like A Giant Lobster Trap

Upon first seeing the wreck, the diver will notice that it has been

10

on the bottom for quite some time. Some of the planking has fallen away leaving gaps which give the wreck an appearance not unlike a giant lobster trap. You can shine a light through the planking and look inside the wreck.

As you swim along the hull you will notice bollards and planking secured to the tug's rotting ribbing with steel rods, washers, and threaded nuts. Anemones add to the sight decorating the wooden surfaces.

Junk Collector
A 4-foot-wide metal plate of unknown origin protrudes 6-8 feet from under the wreck.

Be careful if you decide to poke around this wreck as it is festooned with old nets and lobster pot accessories.

Visibility Problems
Visibility at the site is usually not spectacular averaging 5 - 15 feet. Remember to stay off the bottom as kicking up silt can reduce visibility to "O".

This site is a great fish attractor as the surrounding bottom is relatively barren. The real strength of this site is in its accessibility.

The barge makes an excellent back-up site when it's too rough to venture out on the open wa-

ter. Being situated between two islands, the site is usually calm enough to get to.

However, even this site is not without hazards. At times, the current can be quite strong. Try to time your dive for slack high water to minimize the current and maximize visibility. The biggest hazard is boat traffic. During the summer months, this waterway is heavily populated with both pleasure and commercial vessels. Make sure that you stay near your boat and fly your dive flag.

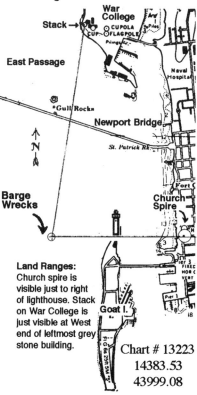

Land Ranges: Church spire is visible just to right of lighthouse. Stack on War College is just visible at West end of leftmost grey stone building.

Chart # 13223
14383.53
43999.08

11

The Luxurious Floating Palace

by Bob Cembrola

- *Empire State*
  Passenger Liner
  Steam Driven, Paddlewheels
  Length 317 feet
- Bristol Harbor
  Independence Park

The Fall River Line

The Fall River Line was formed in 1847. It operated luxurious "floating palaces" from Fall River, Massachusetts to New York City with a stop in Newport Rhode Island. A railroad link with Boston brought passengers and cargo to the dock where the Battleship *Massachusetts* now sits in the Taunton River.

Impressive Dimensions

The *Empire State* was built for the Fall River Line by Lawrence & Sneeden of New York and launched in 1848. She had 106 staterooms with 500 berths on the lower deck. Her impressive dimensions were: length 317 feet; breadth over the guards: 79 feet; 39 foot breadth over the hull; depth of hold: 13.5 feet and 1600 tons displacement. Her paddle wheels were 38 feet in diameter with buckets 10.25 feet long.

The Jinxed Palace

She was originally called *Plymouth Rock* but before launching was renamed *Empire State*, an act some believed jinxed her.

Indeed, less than a year after beginning service she burnt at the dock in Fall River on January 13, 1849. The hull was raised and towed to New York for repairs at the then exorbitant cost of $200,000.

In 1857 she sank near Hell Gate and the next year struck a rock about 30 miles from New York City and sank again. On both occasions she was repaired and put back in service.

During the Civil War she trans-

12

ported soldiers to New York who were destined for some of the bloodiest battles of that conflict.

After the War, the *Newport & Old Colony* joined the Fall River Line and the *Empire State* was relegated to the role of spare boat. In 1871 she was sold to the Bay State Boat Company which used her for excursion trips in the Northeast including one to Philadelphia for the Centennial Exposition in June of 1876.

Torched At Bristol
On May 14, 1887 while at the dock in Bristol, she was the victim of an arsonist who did his job well; she could not be resuscitated this time. Her boilers, engines and other usable gear were salvaged by the owners, her charred hulk left to settle in the silt of Bristol harbor.

The next serious salvage effort took place in the 1960's when Jackson Jenks, a diver, who was also director of his own Naval and Maritime Museum in Newport, Rhode Island, removed a good deal of material which he felt had value. The museum is no longer in existence.

Locating The *Empire State*
The remains of the *Empire State* lie just off Independence Park in Bristol Harbor. Look for the rock pile and red can #6 less than 100 yards from the boardwalk. The wreckage is scattered about near the rock pile.

Diving The *Empire State*
The *Empire State* is one of the easiest wreck dives in Rhode Island in terms of access and depth.

This is an an excellent site to view the destructive effects of man and nature on a mostly wooden ship. Despite the lethal wounds inflicted by the fire and salvage work, there is still enough of her carcass to entertain all but the most brass hungry diver.

Although a good percentage of her remains are buried under silt, the massiveness of her floor timbers and keelson is readily apparent. Pipes of various sizes and functions jut out in seemingly random fashion in mute testimony to a once proud and opulent "floating palace" where millionaires sipped tea under chandeliers and immigrants from Europe began the second leg of the journey bringing them to their new homes.

Take Every Precaution
Many boats cut between the rock pile and the wall, especially at high tide—**Always** use a dive flag. Fishermen use the boardwalk—stay clear of their hooks!

The *Explorer*

by **Steven Dumas**

- *Explorer*
- Wooden trawler
  Western-rigged, stern trawler
  Diesel driven, single screw
  Length 62 feet, Beam 18.8 feet
- Newport — Sheep Point
  2 NM south
  Chart # 13223
- 14385.9
  43971.1
- 14386.3
  43971.4

The Trap

During several months of the year, the Coast Guard designates certain areas along the Rhode Island coast as fish trap areas. See chart # 13223.

The floating fish traps are supported by 55 gallon stainless steel drums.

Ships Specifications

The *Explorer* was a 62-foot-long wooden, western-rigged stern trawler. She was built in 1978 by Vernon Lewis of Hampstead, North Carolina. Her stainless steel masts and rigging stood 30 feet above the deck.

A single Detroit diesel Model 8v92 engine supplied propulsion to the *Explorer's* single massive prop. Auxiliary power was supplied by a four-cylinder Northern Lights diesel engine.

The Disaster

What began as a routine day of fishing on Friday, June 26, 1994 turned ugly at 7:30 p.m.

Captain Joseph Roque of Charlestown, Rhode Island, an experienced fisherman, was navigating the *Explorer* in the waters 1.5 NM south of Aquidneck Island.

The *Explorer* lurched violently when her massive four-blade prop impaled one of the Coast Canning Corporation's 55 gallon stainless steel drums. The impaled drum was driven by the prop through the *Explorer's* stern.

She quickly lost her battle with the water pouring into her hold and descended, upright, 90 feet to the ocean floor.

Just before she sank, Captain Roque and crew boarded the life raft and abandoned ship. They were rescued by the Coast Guard a short time later.

The Dive

When diving a wreck as well-preserved and intact as the Explorer was in 1994, the diver **must** be constantly aware of the overhead environment.

The massive mast and outriggers tower 50 feet above the ocean floor to within 40 feet of the surface. An abundance of marine life is seen clinging to cables and rigging that clutter the wreck.

The Explorer is listing 30 degrees to starboard as she sits upright on the ocean floor. The decks of the wreck are littered with the remains of fishing gear once used on the boat. On both sides of the wheelhouse are the hydraulic deck winches used to haul in the huge fishing net.

Moving aft on the boat, the large drum on which the net was rolled while underway will be seen. With out-riggers resting in their lowered position, it is easy to imagine the ship engaged in fishing.

Penetration of the wreck is possible; however this should only be attempted by the most experienced wreck divers. In the wheelhouse lie the vast array of electronics, encrusted by corrosion.

Below deck, astern, is a large fishhold that may be entered by way of a stern deck hatch. Amidships, the large diesel engines that powered the vessel are seen under the galley.

Below the bow bit is the forward locker which was used for the storage of nets and line. There is a large square deck hatch that makes this compartment easily accessible. The diver must be very cautious when penetrating below decks. Many lines and pieces of net still float free in the hold.

Dropping off the deck to the ocean floor, the Explorer's prop can still be seen partially buried below the silt. The hole punched by the stainless drum is visible on the port side just above the prop. One learns respect for the might of the ocean after seeing how such a small breach in the hull can claim a vessel so quickly.

A Legal Note

At the time of publication, the Explorer was still owned by Captain Joseph R. Roque, Charlestown, Rhode Island. Gathering artifacts was illegal.

Exciting Newport Dive Sites

by Marlene & Don Snyder

1. Van Zandt Pier

Van Zandt Pier is located immediately south of the Newport Bridge, at the intersection of Van Zandt Avenue and Washington Street, where there is limited public parking.

Walk to the end of the pier and down the steps into the water. Many bottles and artifacts from earlier times may be seen. This is a shallow dive with a maximum depth of 25 feet.

2. Fort Adams

From Ocean Drive, enter Fort Adams State Park. Follow the sign to the Eisenhower House. Drive past the house to the East Passage where there are several easy entry points.

Diving and subsea visibility are best in this location at slack tide with a southerly wind. Depths are from 40 feet near the shore to over 150 feet in the shipping channel. The bottom is rocky, with a great variety of marine life.

3. Pirate's Cove—Brenton State Park

On Ocean Drive watch for a white guard rail on the ocean side just 2/10 of a mile north of the entrance to Brenton Point State Park. Drop off your equipment and diving partner at the guard rail, leave your vehicle in the Park and walk back to your equipment.

On the beach, orient yourself with your back to a large rock in the center of the cove, looking across the Bay at Beavertail lighthouse on the southern tip of Jamestown.

To your right, the bottom is mostly sandy; there you can encounter horseshoe crabs, rays, and flounder.

To your left the bottom is rocky, with brown kelp; there you are likely to see many of the local varieties of fish, cunner, tautog and flatfish. The remains of a sunken ship, timbers, and an anchor are scattered in the area. Maximum depth is 40 feet. Winds from the south can hamper visibility.

4. Ruggles Avenue

Located just south of the Breakers mansion, off Bellevue Avenue, this right-of-way ends at the historic Cliff Walk.

Observe all parking regulations.

Climb down a steep embankment to reach a magnificent diving location which combines a rocky and sandy bottom with depths to 25 feet. Take care, this can be a turbulent entry.

Newport Dive Site Locations

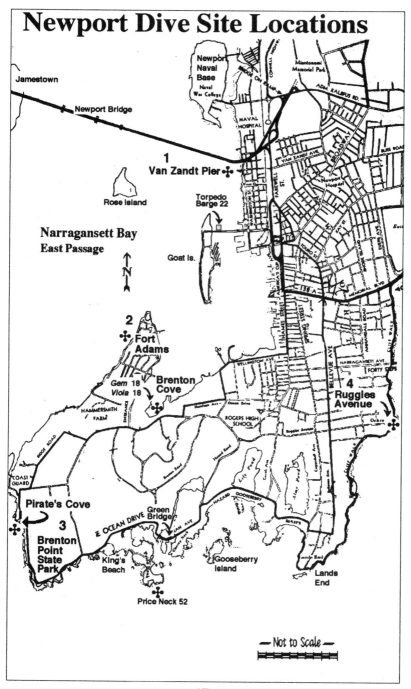

Jamestown

Newport Bridge

Newport Naval Base
Naval War College

Newport Naval Base
Naval College

Miantonomi Memorial Park

ADM. KALBFUS RD.

NAVAL HOSPITAL

1
Van Zandt Pier ⚓

Rose Island

Torpedo Barge 22

VAN ZANDT AVE.

BROADWAY

Newport Hospital

BLISS ROAD

Narragansett Bay East Passage

↑N

Goat Is.

FAREWELL ST.

SPRING STREET

THAMES STREET

MEMORIAL BLVD.

2
⚓ Fort Adams

Gem 18
Viola 18

Brenton Cove ⚓

WELLINGTON AVE.

HAMMERSMITH FARM

Harrison Ave. · Ocean Drive

ROGERS HIGH SCHOOL

BELLEVUE AVE

NARRAGANSETT AVE.

FORTY STEPS

4
Ruggles Avenue

Ochre ⚓

COAST GUARD

ROCK ROAD

Pirate's Cove

3
⚓
Brenton Point State Park

E. OCEAN DRIVE

Green Bridge

King's Beach

Lily Pond

HAZARD

GOOSEBERRY

Gooseberry Island

Lands End

⚓
Price Neck 52

— Not to Scale —

17

Fort Adams' Slave Ship & Rum Runner

by Marlene & Don Snyder

- Bark *Gem* & Rum Runner *Viola* • Newport—Chart# 13223
  Brenton Cove—Fort Adams

The Newport Slave Trade

Rhode Island's first major commercial enterprise was the gruesome rum-slaves-sugar and molasses "triangle trade."

During the 1600's, schooners—Guinea ships—loaded with casks of Rhode Island rum, sailed from Newport to Africa's slave coast on the Gulf of Guinea.

In Africa the enterprising captains traded the rum to African coastal tribes for gold and slaves.

The ships then sailed to the West Indies, where the captains bartered the slaves to the West Indians for sugar and molasses.

The ships completed the triangle by returning to Newport where the sugar and molasses were used to distill more rum.

The Newport Slavers

In 1698 England rescinded the *Royal African Company's* monopoly making it legal for Rhode Island merchants to import slaves directly from Africa.

Nearly 20 percent of the slaves died on the wretched ships. Those who survived were auctioned off and used as farm hands and domestics in the homes of wealthy Rhode Islanders.

In 1774 it became illegal to ship slaves to Rhode Island. Nonetheless, the smuggling of slaves continued until the beginning of the Civil War, 1861.

The Slaver *Gem*

The Bark *Gem* was wrecked on the west shore of Block Island on January 6, 1856.

The February 9, 1856 edition of the *Newport Mercury* reported that the *Gem* "was built at Baltimore about four years since; is of superior model for sailing and built of the best natural material; 350 tons register, copper fastened."

The *Mercury* also reported that the *Gem* had been returning to New York from the west coast of Africa with a "cargo of Ivory, Ebony, Palm oil, etc."

It has been speculated that the *Gem's* master, Captain J. D. Northam, was involved in the smuggling of slaves.

After she was wrecked the *Gem* was towed to Newport. After first trying without success to refloat her, and then to auction her, Captain Northam abandoned her at Crandall's Wharf, Newport.

Brenton Cove

The Crandall Wharf proprietors finally had the *Gem* towed to the Fort Adams shore of Newport's Brenton Cove, where she remained until her destruction by the 1938 hurricane.

Diving The *Gem*

Most of the remains of the *Gem* lie buried under the sand, parallel to the base of the Fort Adams boat ramp. Some scattered timbers and a 12 foot section of the hull are visible. Copper spikes and fastenings may be observed.

Diving The Rum Runner *Viola*

East from the boat ramp, across Brenton Cove, approximately 200 yards, on the opposite shore, is a deteriorating dock. Under the pilings of the dock, in 8-10 feet of water are the remains of a wooden vessel known by local divers as the Rum Runner *Viola*.

John Stanford, an avid wreck diver, marine researcher, and author, reports that the *Viola* was a steam driven screw yacht, with one deck, two masts, and an elliptical stern. Her specifications were: Length 108.6 feet, Beam 16.1 feet, Draft 8.7 feet, Weight 53.44 tons. She was built in South Boston in 1895 of wood beam construction, fastened with iron pins. How she ended up on the bottom of Brenton Cove is a mystery.

The *Viola's* bow faces south. Her port side is partially buried in sand. Follow the hull under the dock 60-70 feet to the stern. The exposed side of the *Viola* rises 4 feet off the bottom.

Map showing: N (north arrow), Brenton Cove, Boat Ramp, *Viola*, Dock, *Gem*

Fastest Boat In The Fleet

by Marlene & Don Snyder

- *George W. Humphreys*
  Wooden fishing steamer
  Length 142.6 feet, Beam 22 feet,
  Depth 18 feet, Gross Tons 214
- Newport Neck
  Brenton Point—.4 NM SW
  Chart # 13223
  14404.68
  43981.24

Gigantic Clawed Hand

Brenton Reef juts out like a gigantic clawed hand from Newport Point, 800 yards southwest into Narragansett Bay's East Passage.

Formed by granite boulders abandoned here 18,000 years ago by a retreating glacier, the reef is littered with the remains of vessels that continue to be entrapped and destroyed by the jagged fingers of granite and the merciless pounding of the sea.

Spanish Brig Sunk Here

On Christmas eve 1810 the Spanish Brig *Minerva* went aground at this same location and was smashed to pieces.

The story of that tragedy is described elsewhere in this book.

George W. Humphreys

On July 6, 1904, nearly 100 years after the *Minerva* was lost here, the steamer *George W. Humphreys*, was fishing for menhaden when she strayed too close to the coast.

Like A Phantom

The *Humphreys* was built in Philadelphia in 1877. She was valued at $10,000. Designed and powered for speed, she immediately earned a reputation as one of the fastest, if not *the* fastest boat in the fleet. Like a phantom, she was out and back with her catch long before the other ships.

Enviable Cash Flow

Driving her as fast as she would go, Captain Church and his crew generated an enviable cash flow for her owners, the

American Fishing Company. She made up for losses sustained by the line's slower vessels and less capable crews.

The Captain Was Wrong

It was nearly 8:30 in the evening and Captain Church was moving at full speed taking advantage of every short-cut to make Newport before dark. Standing at the pilot house window, he was certain of his course because he could hear the Brenton Reef Light Ship's signal.

The Captain was wrong! The *Humphreys* came to a smashing halt stuck fast in shallow water between the two reefs located approximately 500 yards northeast of Gong R"4".

Captain Strips Ship

Captain Church and the crew left the ship in a lifeboat. The Captain returned in the American Fishing Company's steamer *Seaconnet* and began stripping the *Humphreys* of everything that was valuable in the event that she could not be saved.

Unable To Lift Steamer

The force of the sea caused the *Humphreys* to be driven from her original position between the reefs to the northern side of the southernmost reef.

The *Humphreys'* new position made it impossible to raise her so that the hole in her hull could be repaired, and she could be hauled off the rock. In the following weeks, the heavy seas broke her in two, smashed her to pieces, and caused her to completely disappear from the face of the sea.

Diving The *Humphreys*

As Chart # 13223 indicates, the **Tide Rips** at this location. Heed the advice—slack tide, flat sea, no surge or else return to port.

What little remains of the *Humphreys* is in 15 feet of water, on the north side of the southernmost reef.

There is a metal structure which may be an engine block with attached drive shaft. The engine block is approximately five feet wide, 10-12 feet long, and 10 feet high. Approximately 4 feet up on the east face of the engine block is what appears to be a 40-foot-long, 30-inch-diameter drive shaft with brass rings at its joints. It slopes to the ocean floor at its eastern end.

Many artifacts are to be found at this location, valves, pipes, cannons from the *Minerva* and the like. The reef is teeming with fish.

21

Goat Island Torpedo Barge

by Marlene & Don Snyder

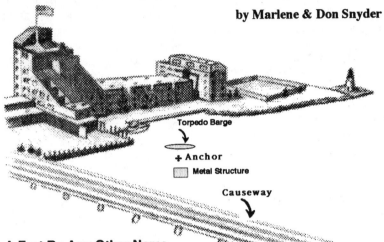

Torpedo Barge

✛ Anchor

▨ Metal Structure

Causeway

A Fort By Any Other Name

The British ordered the construction of a small earthen battery on Goat Island in 1700. Enlarged and named Fort Anne in 1702, it was renamed Fort George in 1730.

Dismantled in 1774, it was rebuilt in 1776 when Rhode Island declared her independence from England, and named Fort Liberty. In 1784 it became Fort Washington and, you guessed it, in 1798 it was rechristened Fort Wolcott.

Strategically Located

Heavy guns strategically located at fortifications on Goat Island, Brenton Point, and Conanicut Island's Dumplings could unleash a triangular volley of death on any enemy vessel foolish enough to enter the bay.

Naval Torpedo Station

In 1799, the Town of Newport turned Goat Island over to the Federal Government. After 70 years of use by the Army it was leased to the Navy for a Torpedo Station in 1869. Its mission was to experimentally develop and manufacture torpedoes and other naval ordnance.

During World War I, depth charges, mines, and torpedoes were produced at the station.

In 1921, Gould Island in the upper East Passage was added to the Torpedo Station. One third of all U.S. World War II torpedoes were produced at the station.

Following World War II the Goat Island Torpedo Station was closed and the island entered a more peaceful era.

A Link to the Mainland

Goat Island was converted from an arsenal to a luxury resort in the 1960s with the construction of a causeway linking it to downtown Newport and the opening of a marina and a luxury hotel.

Diving Goat Island

An excellent place to start this **boat dive** is in the cove between the northern tip of the island and the causeway. The cove is protected from the wind and waves.

This location is very close to the shore and to the hotel which are private property—please respect the privacy and rights of the tourists and fishermen so that divers will continue to be welcome here.

It is essential that a diver's flag be prominently displayed so that motor craft and sailboats, with their silent lethal metal keels, will stay clear.

Off the dining room and boat slip, in 25 feet of water, are the remains of a metal barge half buried in the silt. The barge is approximately 15 feet wide and 50 feet long. Its sides rise 2-3 feet off the bottom.

South of the barge approximately 200 feet are the remains of a yet-to-be-identified metal structure, about 15 feet at the base which rises 10 feet toward the surface.

Between the barge and the metal structure is an anchor with a shank around 6 feet in length.

Recently deposited cocktail glasses, wine goblets, and water glasses are frequently retrieved here. An ancient onion bottle was found under the causeway.

Historically Significant Site

Goat Island was a military fortification and an arsenal for 300 years. The waters surrounding this tiny island are littered with artifacts and shipwrecks. See the *British Warships*' articles and charts in this book.

Torpedo Run by Marlene & Don Snyder

- Gould Island

Torpedoes Away!

During World War I Gould Island was activated as a naval high explosive storage facility and placed under the jurisdiction of the Commander of the Goat Island Naval Torpedo Station.

In 1921, a seaplane hangar and water ramp were constructed to facilitate two anti-submarine warfare seaplanes deployed to the Island for the purpose of airdropping experimental torpedoes.

From a World War I civilian work force of 927, the Gould Island facility mushroomed to 12,600 men and women during World War II. The civilians worked 24 hours a day, 7 days a week, and produced one third of the torpedoes used by the Navy during the war years.

In addition to the seaplanes, a blimp was assigned to Gould Island in 1944 to monitor test-fired torpedoes.

Torpedoes Still Fired There

Although the southern two-thirds of Gould Island is state land, the Navy still maintains a very active torpedo firing facility at the north end of the Island. The unarmed torpedoes are propelled by compressed air or compressed water. Their warheads carry instruments instead of explosives.

Torpedo Sinks Fishing Boat

In 1951, the 30-foot fishing boat, *On Time*, was sunk by an unarmed torpedo between Gould Island and Jamestown. Reliable sources report that unretrieved torpedoes still remain in and close to the firing range area.

To replicate the weapons systems of surface ships, torpedoes are fired from tubes protruding through open doors in the Torpedo Station. To duplicate a submarine launch, other tubes are mounted on elevators so that they can be lowered into the bay and their torpedoes fired underwater.

The firing range stretches for five nautical miles north up the bay. It is clearly marked on Chart #13223 as a military area, imprinted with the words: PROHIBITED AREA 334.80.

Although all firings are unscheduled, ominous-looking gray patrol boats clear the firing range of vessels before each firing.

Diving Gould Island
Gould Island is a fascinating diving and spearfishing location which drops off very rapidly on both the east and west sides.

Diving these steep sides is often rewarding to the patient diver who is in search of marine life or artifacts from the war years. The bottom tends to be flat and sandy with few rocks.

Another gratifying dive is in the cove on the northeast tip of the Island formed by the

Torpedo Launcher

Cove

Dol

N

24
Foul

Obstr

Gould Island

F

East Passage
Between Conanicut
& Aquidnick Islands
Chart # 13223

wood pilings protruding east into the bay from the elevator torpedo launching tubes.

At slack tide, anchor your boat in the cove near the pilings. The water in the cove is about 20 feet deep out to the lighted marker.

Extraordinary Spearfishing
The outside of the pilings is an extraordinarily good spot for spearfishing.

For some reason known only to them, huge tautog can be had here before they become readily available in other parts of the bay.

When they are running, huge stripers and bluefish swim by as if in a shooting gallery. You can have your pick of the largest.

This is a spot also known to boat fishermen. Observe all of the precautions— diver's flag, changing tide, casting fishermen, boat props, etc.

Like A Shipwreck
Running the length and width of the wood pilings is a tangle of metal girders resembling the superstructure of a sunken ship.

The jumbled mass of girders rises nearly to the surface in spots. It is a diving location well worth the trip.

Hellcat Vanishes Into The Sea

by George A. Flynn,
    Article & Graphics

First Person Account

Author's Note: Lawrence D. Webster, an aircraft archeologist, provided technical information for this article and the identity of the pilot. The pilot, Tom Delehaunty, described the crash to the author during telephone conversations in January 1995.

The Adventure Begins

On October 21, 1945, Lt. JG Thomas Delehaunty was flying the Hellcat off Block Island, Rhode Island when he noticed a wisp of smoke coming from his engine — could be an oil leak! He coolly followed Navy procedures and signaled to his wingman in the F4U Corsair to come alongside and escort him back to Quonset Point field.

By the time they were within sight of Point Judith, conditions had badly deteriorated. The leak had become a gusher and oil pressure had dropped dangerously low. Lt. Delehaunty immediately radioed ground control and was instructed to try to land at Charlestown Air Base. Before he could turn into his final approach, the engine froze up. He had no choice but to make a water landing and fast.

No Stranger to Danger

Lt. Delehaunty was no stranger to crises situations. He had previously "put one in" near Chappaquiddick Island and in the previous year, while in the Pacific, he was forced to make a crash landing into the barrier of an aircraft carrier.

He felt fairly confident of his chances because he was flying the rugged F6F Hellcat, the Navy's finest fighter plane. Back in the Pacific, he had seen one "take a hit" and, with a six foot hole in it, land safely on a carrier. The plane's durability was legendary among pilots.

Luck of the Irish

Fortunately the water was fairly calm with very little wind. He maneuvered the fighter so it paralleled the beach, but beyond the surf line, and on a chilly October afternoon, Lt. Tom Delehaunty, traveling at 60 knots with his wheels up, made a classic water landing. It was not much rougher than a hard carrier landing — like skipping a stone over the surface of the water.

Initially, the plane's nose went under because of the engine's weight, but it immediately bobbed up again due to the plane's buoyancy. Delehaunty quickly unstrapped his shoulder harness, exited the cockpit, inflated his Mae West, and swam over 100 yards to shore.

Now You See It, Now You Don't

Delehaunty was to receive two more "booster shots" before the day ended. One from the ambulance crew that picked him up and the other at the Naval hospital where he was examined. The Navy takes care of its own!

He was soon brought back to reality. When he arrived home that evening, his wife chided him for being late. She thought he had stopped to play basketball. The following morning, his commanding officer, while solici-

He was greeted by a local fisherman who had witnessed the entire drama. After assuring himself that the young pilot was safe and sound, and giving him a restorative shot of whiskey, the fisherman then focused his interest on how he might salvage the plane's tires for his Model T Ford, rubber being scarce because of the war. When he scanned the water to confirm the plane's location, the Hellcat had disappeared.

tous of his health and well-being, was more than a little perturbed that he had lost a plane equipped with top secret landing gear. He promptly sent him off with five other men, armed with grappling hooks and a dory, to find the plane. They spent the rest of the day searching to no avail.

The Hellcat Had Vanished
As described in the following article, the Hellcat would not be seen again for thirty years.

Scuba Diver Finds Hellcat

by George A. Flynn, Article & Graphics

Thirty Years Later

After sinking in 1945 it would be close to thirty years before the Hellcat would again make an appearance.

Six presidents would serve; the Korean and Vietnam Wars would be fought; man would walk on the moon; Elvis would come and go (or maybe not); and Cousteau would invent the Scuba System.

Scuba Diver Finds Hellcat

About 1974 or '75, a lobsterman, working his pots, snagged his line on a submerged object. Pulling proved futile so he offered a nearby diver a few lobsters if he could work it loose.

The diver, George Skovron, followed the line down and was greeted with a once-in-a-lifetime sight. The Hellcat had been found! It was nearly perfectly preserved as if in a museum.

The cruel sea

Over the intervening years the ocean and men have taken a heavy toll on the once formidable fighter plane. Storms and tides have covered it with sand and uncovered it countless times.

The corrosive action of salt water has eaten away at its vulnerable parts. The engine has separated from the fuselage and is not to be found at the immediate site. The wings and tail assembly are gone, possibly washed ashore somewhere over the years or taken further out by draggers.

Shell fishermen and seaclammers have pulled up pieces of the fuselage and cockpit. Divers have taken souvenirs. All that remains to be seen is the aluminum framework of the fuselage, where a large, moody looking tautog has taken up residence. He leaves when divers arrive and reclaims ownership when they depart. Undoubtedly, there are still parts of the plane beneath the sand.

Diving the Hellcat
It is not an easy wreck to find. At times, divers have missed it completely or have spent twenty minutes to a half hour locating it. Because of this, it is not an overly frequented wreck.

Line of sight landmarks are the most reliable means of putting yourself in close vicinity. Visibility can be fair or difficult depending on tides and weather conditions. There are scatterings of rocks and vegetation that can confuse the search. At a distance, the fuselage could be mistaken for one of these.

The plane lies about 100 yards off the beach to the right of the Breachway. It rests in twenty feet of water and faces North.

Epilogue
After his Quonset Point assignment, Tom flew as a test pilot in Jacksonville, Florida for the remainder of his Naval career. His son is also a Navy pilot. He has been extremely helpful in sharing his experience.

His willingness and generous attitude have been invaluable in filling out the details of this fascinating story. In telephone conversations with Tom, he "sounds" like a fighter pilot — sharp as a tack and with total recall. He gives the impression that he could fire up a Hellcat at a moment's notice and fly off into the wild blue yonder.

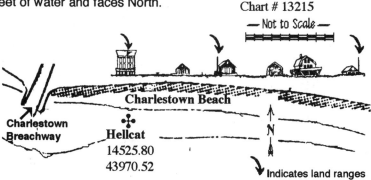

Chart # 13215
— Not to Scale —

Charlestown Beach

Charlestown Breachway

Hellcat
14525.80
43970.52

N

Indicates land ranges

29

Hercules' Final Labor

by Marlene & Don Snyder with Captain Bill Palmer

- **Tug *Hercules***
- Wooden tugboat
  Steam screw driven
  108 feet long, Beam 22 feet
  155 tons
- Misquamicut State Beach
- Chart # 13215
  14594.11
  43971.11
- Depth 15 feet

War Duty

The *Hercules* was one of the most famous tugs on the east coast. She was chartered by the New York Herald newspaper and went to Cuba to cover one of this country's shortest conflicts, the Spanish-American War, April-December 1898.

Among her exploits, the *Hercules* enabled the Herald's correspondents to scoop the other tabloids with the news that the American Navy had destroyed the Spanish fleet at Santiago, Cuba on July 3, 1898.

The Final Voyage Begins

The *Hercules* had recently been overhauled at a price of $17,000. She was in excellent shape when her final voyage began at 7:00 a.m., December 12, 1907.

As the tug left Newport bound for New London with four manned barges in tow, Captain H. W. Stevens observed that: "The sea was running moderately, and there was apparently no difficulty before us in making a safe running." A total of 16 crew members manned the 5 vessels. The wife of one of the crew was also along as a passenger.

A Race Against Death

By noon the powerful tug *Hercules* with her four barges in tow had passed Weekapaug Point. Without warning they were engulfed in a northeaster with 65-mile-an-hour gale force winds, blinding snow, and 15 foot high seas.

Captain and crew were thrown about like match sticks when

something huge and sinister seemingly rose from the depths of the violent sea and impaled the bottom of their vessel. It seemed to sink and rise again, penetrating her a second time. The pumps were immediately overwhelmed by the water pouring in through the gaping wounds in her hull.

Captain Stevens signaled the barges to drop their anchors, and then cut them loose. He immediately turned the drowning tug toward shore, threw her powerful engines to full throttle, and in a race against death, ran her aground, 100 yards offshore, just as the engines died and the water washed over her.

Coast Guard To The Rescue
Captain and crew were able to reach shore in two lifeboats. They then walked 10 miles to the Watch Hill Coast Guard station. Miraculously everyone on the barges was rescued by the Coast Guard.

At first it was speculated that the *Hercules* had hit the floating remains of the *Larchmont,* wrecked just offshore the previous February, or the schooner *John Paull,* wrecked near there in 1893.

It was later determined that the *Hercules* had been blown off course by the storm and struck

Old Reef—see Chart# 13215— just offshore from where Captain Stevens beached her.

Finding The *Hercules*
The remains of the *Hercules* are strewn about the flat sandy bottom of Misquamicut State Beach, in 15 feet of water approximately 100 yards offshore, just beyond the swimming area.

Come in on the numbers when the ocean is flat and you can see the bottom. With the bow of the boat pointed at the sand dunes, with the Town Beach pavilion to starboard and Old Reef at the stern, the dark, straight lines of the wreck should be visible on the sandy bottom running parallel, east and west, to the beach.

Diving The *Hercules*
When the water is clear and the ocean calm, you will experience some of the most interesting diving in Rhode Island.

The scattered remains of the *Hercules* include a 70-foot-long drive shaft, a prop protruding from the sand, and part of the stern section which rises 10 feet above the floor of the ocean, with an opening large enough to swim through.

Captain Bill Roe, who discovered the *Hercules*, advises that there are still artifacts buried in the sand.

31

Pursuing The Prey

by Marlene & Don Snyder with John Warszawski

- *Heroine*
- Fishing trawler
- Steel, steam driven
  Length 100+ feet
- Chart # 13215
- Charlestown Breachway
  3.5 NM south
  14525.7
  43945.9
- Depth 70 feet

Plundering The Sea

Colonists arriving on the Rhode Island coast discovered a cornucopia, seemingly overflowing with an unlimited supply of fish, shellfish, waterfowl, and mammals. Lobsters could be collected at low tide. Oysters, soft-shelled clams, scallops, quahogs, and lobsters—all free for the taking.

They could stand in Rhode Island's coastal waters with seines, large hand-held nets, and catch as many fish as they required: menhaden, bluefish, scup, squid, butterfish, and other fish.

Enough Is Never Enough

By the early 1800's hand-held seines could not provide enough bounty to satisfy the insatiable hunger of the burgeoning population.

Floating Fish Traps

In the late 1800's hook-and-line and seines were replaced by floating and staked fish traps. Between 1880 and 1910 the number of these highly efficient fish traps staked around the Bay and on the south shore had risen from 166 to 400.

The resulting decimation of fish populations, coupled with pressure on Congress by hook-and-line and seine fishermen eventually resulted in drastic fish trap restrictions. Today there are no floating traps in the Bay and the few remaining traps are off the Newport shore, in the Sakonnet River, and along the Narragansett coast.

Trawlers

In the early 1900's trawlers or "draggers," as they were called in Rhode Island, replaced fish traps. Operating in the Bay and Sound, they towed a funnel-shaped net over the seabed scooping up bottom fish. More efficient and effective than the fish traps that they had replaced, the dragger's nets, of today, select out only the legally allowed bottom dwelling fish.

Abandon Ship!
Captain Bonia and his crew of 28 men had steamed up from New York on June 18, 1920 to trawl for fish in Block Island Sound.

Sometime during the night the *Heroine* sprung a leak. As dawn arrived captain and crew realized that the situation was hopeless and took to the life-boats just moments before the rising water reached the *Heroine's* firebox.

Abandoned by her captain and crew, her fires extinguished, the powerless *Heroine* disappeared beneath the sea. She rested there, alone and undisturbed for four decades.

The *Rose Of Italy*
A short time after abandoning ship, Captain Bonia and his crew were picked up by The *Rose of Italy*, a fishing boat, and taken to Newport. They stayed overnight at the Army and Navy Y.M.C.A. Captain and crew re-turned to New York the next day.

Diving The *Heroine*
Wreck diver John Warszawski, Jamestown Rhode Island, provided the following information.

Although pretty well demolished, the *Heroine* is recognizable as a shipwreck. The ravages of time, turbulence, and possibly draggers have demolished and scattered the once intact hull.

When the *Heroine* sank, her wheelhouse came apart from the wreck and has never been found.

The *Heroine* is changing over time. She is now largely broken up. The stern and center section are crushed down and scattered to the south. Piles of debris rise in some places 20 feet off the bottom.

Years ago the bow section was upright and the deck was flat with a big anchor sitting on it. In September 1991 Hurricane Bob wreaked havoc on the Rhode Island coast and portions of its undersea terrain. The once up-right bow now faces east and lists 60° to starboard. The anchor slid off the deck and sits upright on the sand leaning against the deck.

It is possible to swim through and inside the intact bow.

Idene—The Hollywood Wreck

by John Stanford

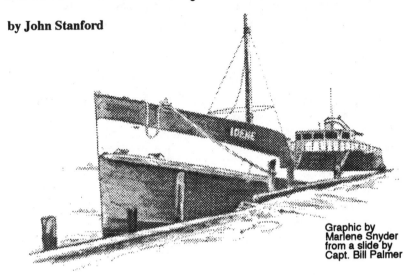

Graphic by
Marlene Snyder
from a slide by
Capt. Bill Palmer

Idene—Steel fishing dragger
Length 120 feet
- Block Island
  Approximately 4 NM south
- Chart # 13205
  14521.6-8
  43851.5

Spectacular Wreck
Approximately 4 nautical miles south of Block Island's Southeast Lighthouse lies one of Rhode Island's newest wrecks, the fishing dragger *Idene*.

Admirable Service
The *Idene* was a 120-foot dragger which hailed from Point Judith for many years.

She did admirable service, dredging fish and clams as far out to sea as the edge of the continental shelf.

The *Idene*, like many other vessels of her type, had helped supply the New England seafood industry for decades.

Deemed Obsolete
At some time, late in her life, she was deemed to be obsolete and was subsequently laid up alongside a wharf in Snug Harbor. For years the *Idene* lay rusting away, an eyesore on the waterfront.

I remember the first time I saw the *Idene* sitting at the dock that I remarked that she would make a great wreck for diving.

Eyesore Scuttled
Evidently someone else had the same idea that I had, as in 1991 the now heavily deteriorated *Idene* was towed to a position

south of Block Island and scuttled.

In just a few short years the *Idene* has been transformed from an eyesore to a great dive site. What was once used to harvest the sea is now providing a life-giving habitat for countless species of marine life.

Finding The *Idene*
The wreck was originally located with side scan sonar and investigated by divers.

Using information provided by the Automated Wreck and Obstruction Information Service (AWOIS) and other sources, my crew and I were able to locate and dive the sunken trawler.

Diving The *Idene*
As you descend the anchor line, you will be greeted by a spectacular sight: a totally intact 120-foot vessel lying upright in 85 feet of water. (Because she is intact, the *Idene* presents a very good target on an average depth finder.)

Swimming from the bow to amidships, the diver will encounter several open hatchways which can be explored. Ladders lead to the now empty cargo holds. These ladders beckon the experienced underwater explorer to enter the lower confines of the vessel.

Amidships there is a very large cargo hatch which provides for easy penetration.

The superstructure and bridge are situated at the stern of the vessel which can be disorienting if you swim behind the superstructure and find yourself at the stern.

All of the recesses and passageways on the bridge can be explored without difficulty. A diver can enter the bridge through one of the side doorways, swim through the interior, and out one of the windows which face forward.

In three short years, marine organisms have done a very respectable job of carpeting the entire wreck with a living cloak. Anemones and colonies of hydroids compete for space over all of the metal surfaces.

I'm sure that the *Idene* attracts tautog and roving schools of pollock, cod and bluefish although the fish-life was quite sparse the first time we dove it.

Hollywood Wreck
This is definitely a "hollywood" wreck, meaning it's intact the way wrecks are often portrayed in movies. Though you probably won't find many artifacts on the *Idene*, she is a very enjoyable dive.

Kettle Bottom Rock — Jamestown

by Dave Shelley

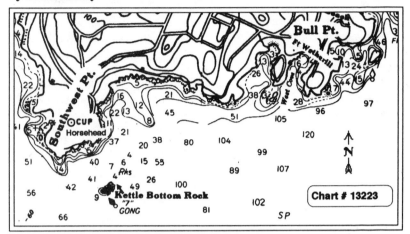

What's in a Name?

The name "Kettle Bottom" appears on charts as far back as the 1700's.

When the reason for the name of a "rock" is elusive do you continue to care or do you entertain one of the following possibilities?

One can easily imagine the first explorers thinking of similar geology in their bays and remarking "that looks just like Kettle Bottom rock."

How about the story of a boat named *Kettle Bottom* finding the rock in less than seamanlike maneuvers and sinking in the process?

Better still, use your imagination coupled with a morsel of history to conjure up your own reason.

Getting To Kettle Bottom

Since the rock is about 1,000 yards from the entrance into the west cove of Fort Wetherill most people would agree that boating to Kettle Bottom is the only way to go.

To find this reef (whether you're looking at a chart or you're on the water) go west, southwest from the Wetherill area. Just south of the rocks is a green "Gong" marked C "7". When deciding on where to anchor take note of the shallow water north of these rocks. Anchoring in this shallow area offers the best holding and a good starting point for the dive.

What's the Current Doing?

Normally you would consult the tide tables and be able to predict current flow. Not at Kettle

Bottom. With deep water on the south and shallow water to the north, the tides can confound the best of us, not so much as to be a hazard, but enough to make us want to pay attention. Most of us would rather float back to the boat instead of swimming up current. Observe the lobster pot buoys in the area to determine the best circuit around the reef.

Fish—Everywhere!

With a little luck the water gods will allow a clockwise route around the rocks. Enter the water and proceed to the northeast point of exposed rocks and descend, then head in a southerly direction looking for a drop off.

After finding the drop off, pick a cruising depth. Usually deep water means bigger fish and a few bugs out looking for dinner. Shallow water yields more light and color. Plenty of the little fish work the face of the wall for whatever dinner comes their way.

Level off, head westerly keeping the wall to the right. Enjoy the show for there is plenty to see. Few places offer so much variety away from the shore crowds. Striped bass can be found cruising, awaiting the unsuspecting bait fish that occasionally school up in the shallows. Tautog munch on the mussels found on

the rocks by day then head down deeper at night looking for a resting place. Lobster, crabs and eels are but a few of the creatures you may happen upon during your dive.

Shipwrecks At Kettle Bottom

The literature is filled with accounts of ships wrecked on Kettle Bottom.

The March 25, 1871 edition of the *Newport Mercury* reported that the Schooner *William James* loaded with granite for the bridge being built to connect New York and Brooklyn, lies on Kettle Bottom Rock. Captain, wife, child, and crew were rescued. Divers then salvaged some of the two ton granite blocks. Artifacts continue to be found at Kettle Bottom.

Go With the Flow

A little more than halfway into your air supply start thinking about turning north to northeast. This may mean ascending to 20 feet or so and going back over the wall.

If Mother Nature cooperates, the reward will be a ride back to the boat. Surfacing at this point to check on your course back to your "chariot" might be prudent. While drifting back to the boat, keep your eyes open for bluefish, striped bass or, in the fall, tropical fish. **Happy diving!**

A Disastrous Mistake

by Marlene & Don Snyder with John Warszawski

- *Lake Crystal*
- Wooden coal barge
- Length 260 feet
  Beam 43 feet
  Height 20+ feet
- Chart # 13215
- Misquamicut
  4 NM south
  14598.4
  43944.9
- Depth 130 feet

Port of Providence

By the early 1800's Providence had become the fourth-largest port in New England.

The boom was about over. A series of wars in Europe had thrown international trade into chaos. Barbary pirates played havoc with American vessels. A changing economy and new laws made Rhode Island's slave trading and profiteering (legalized pirating) illegal and, more importantly, unprofitable.

By 1946, Rhode Island's shipping had been relegated to a small coastal trade bringing in coal, lumber, and petroleum.

Delivering The Goods

The Cullen Transportation Company of New York had a long-standing reputation for always delivering the goods when other carriers were too timid to venture out into the storm.

It was not surprising that The Cullen Company was commissioned to transport two barges of soft coal from Edgewater, New Jersey to the New England Coal and Coke Company in Providence, Rhode Island, even though the weather bureau had forecast winds of gale force velocity and high seas.

The two mammoth barges, each loaded with 3,500 tons of soft coal, would be towed by the Cullen Transportation Company's tug *Nottingham*.

The *Nottingham* was commanded by an experienced master, Captain Gunner Broadwick. Eight seamen manned the *Lake Crystal*.

They Vanished One By One

At first light on Wednesday, February 13, 1946 the *Nottingham* got underway with the two barges in tow. The day dawned leaden and frigid— the empty sea was dead calm. The vessels vanished, one by one over the horizon.

A Disastrous Mistake

As the *Nottingham* proceeded up the coast, the wind began to increase and the sea to run higher. Captain Broadwick dropped one of the barges at New London Wednesday night. Even though the wind had now reached gale force velocity and the sea was running high, Captain Broadwick set off for Providence with the *Lake Crystal* heaving violently in tow— a disastrous mistake.

Battered To Pieces

As dawn broke on Valentine's day, Thursday, February 14th, Captain Broadwick saw the *Lake Crystal's* blinker light signaling for help—but it was too late. The eight crew members, none of whom could swim, had been forced to pile into a life raft just as the heavily-laden wooden coal barge was torn apart by the raging sea, and sank. The gale force winds and mountainous seas immediately capsized the life raft. Of the eight man crew, only the 41-year-old cook survived. The bodies of six others were recovered. The body of the eighth man was never recovered.

Diving The *Lake Crystal*

Up until 1991 the 260-foot-long *Lake Crystal* was lying nearly upside down in 130 feet of water. There was 20 feet of space between the ocean floor and her gunnel. It was possible to get underneath the barge and swim up inside.

As a result of Hurricane Bob in September 1991 and a Halloween night northeaster that same year, the barge is silted-up to within 3 feet of the gunnel.

Although there used to be a lot more to see, this is still a great example of an intact deep water wreck.

Holes in the stern are now covered. Port holes that were once nearly visible are buried. Scuppers that were 10-15 feet up on the bow are now waist high. It is still possible to penetrate through holes in the bow.

Many dishes bearing the Ford Motor Company logo have been found on the barge.

Another violent storm may uncover the barge again or bury her completely.

Beware of the currents in this area.

39

Man Escapes Watery Grave

by Marlene & Don Snyder, with Captain Bill Roe and John Warszawski

- *Mary Arnold*
  Tug boat, 70 feet long
- Chart # 13215
- Charlestown Breachway
  1.5 NM south
- 14530.2 — 43962.0

- **Barge** *Progress*
- 14530.1 — 43961.3

His First And Last Trip
Interviewed in his hospital bed, Everett Dufresne, age 24, told the following story.

A Storm Was Building
It was shortly before midnight, Wednesday, November 24, 1940. The tug boat *Mary Arnold* was towing a large flat bottom barge called a lighter, and the dredger *Progress* from Greenwich, Connecticut to Riverside, Rhode Island to do a dredging job for the Gulf Refining Company.

Captain Sanford and 5 seamen were on the *Mary Arnold*. The *Progress* was manned by Everett Dufresne and three seamen, none of whom had been at sea before. The two Thibeault brothers were on the lighter.

A storm was building and Cap-

tain Sanford decided to have the boats drop anchor 1.5 NM south of the Charlestown breakwater and wait until it passed.

Lurching Drunkenly
Everett Dufresne, who had been seasick since leaving port, said that the *Progress* was lurching drunkenly. Half filled with water, the *Progress* was suddenly capsized by a monstrous wave and sank. Fortunately, Everett and his three companions were thrown clear before the dredger sank. Emil Wydler, the only one not wearing a life preserver, was never seen again.

Everett was in the raging sea for nearly 60 terror packed minutes. Just as he grasped a rope thrown to him by the Thibeaults from the lighter, a wave sucked him underneath the lighter, smashing his head into the keel. He was finally pulled aboard.

When the *Mary Arnold* came alongside the lighter the Thibeault brothers refused to leave. The two men rescued with Everett jumped aboard the pitching tug. When Everett jumped, he missed and landed in the ocean. It took the crew 15 minutes to drag him aboard the tug. He immediately fell asleep in the engine room.

When the Coast Guard Cutter *Argo* arrived from Newport, Captain Sanford indicated that the *Mary Arnold* and the lighter could ride out the storm. The *Argo* returned to Newport.

Within the hour Everett Dufresne was jarred awake by the command "Abandon Ship!"— the *Mary Arnold* was sinking.

Just before she capsized and sank, the *Progress* had smashed into the tug, perhaps causing the leak that later sank the *Mary Arnold*.

To The Lifeboat
Captain Sanford and his crew bailed and rowed their leaking lifeboat toward a faint light which emerged and disappeared in the distance as their boat rose and fell with each wave. They reached the Point Judith breakwater at dawn.

The Coast Guard Cutter *Argo* towed the lighter, crewed by the Thibeault brothers, to Newport.

Everett Dufresne concluded: "That was the first time I was ever on a boat and you can bet it is going to be the last, too!"

Diving The *Mary Arnold*
The *Mary Arnold's* bow has collapsed and the deck is level with the sand.

The most recognizable features include the remains of a small upright boiler and a protruding drive shaft 15-20 feet long. At the end of the drive shaft is a steel prop.

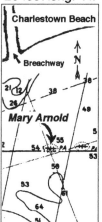

The boiler and drive shaft are surrounded by debris and wreckage.

Diving The *Progress*
Approximately 100 yards southeast of the *Mary Arnold* are the scattered remains of the much larger *Progress*. It is a very interesting dive.

Although the wooden dredger has fallen apart, there is much machinery left. Artifacts are still found on the wreck.

Excursion To Eternity

by Marlene & Don Snyder with Captain Bill Palmer

- *Metis*
- Misquamicut—3.5 NM south
- Chart # 13215
- 14594.58(6)
  43948.76(6)
  25971.1
- Depth130 feet

A Profit Making Trip

On Thursday, August 29th, 1872, the captain of the *Metis,* Charles L. Burton, supervised as the crew piled cargo into the hold, and onto the deck, carelessly covering the hatchways.

The *Metis* had been converted from a freighter to a passenger ship by The Providence and New York Steamship Company eight years before. She was a 200-foot-long, 1,238 ton, propeller-driven wooden steamer.

In addition to a cargo overload, the *Metis* had been purposely overbooked with passengers to squeeze every cent of profit possible from the summer's-end trip to Providence, Rhode Island.

One hundred and seven unsuspecting men, women, and children streamed aboard.

Through Hell Gate

As night descended, the *Metis*, accompanied by another New York Steamship Company boat, the *Nereus*, continued down New York's East River and through Hell Gate on her trip to eternity.

What had begun as a calm trip changed radically as light rain became a blinding deluge. The wind raged into a howling gale whipping the ocean into towering mountains of water.

Collision Course

At 3 a.m. the *Metis* was five miles southeast of Watch Hill. Without warning, a ship appeared out of the pitch black, seething ocean and impaled her thirty feet from the port bow.

The two-masted sailing schoo-

42

ner *Nettie Cushing*, a fraction of the size of the *Metis,* was bound from Providence to New York.

Propelled by a gale force wind, her belly full of rock-heavy lime, the *Cushing* drove her jib boom deep into the *Metis.*

Her pleas to the *Metis* for help ignored, the *Cushing* made it to harbor without a loss of life.

A Gross Error
The crew negligently determined that there was no serious damage to the *Metis* and signaled the *Nereus* to continue alone to Providence–a gross error in judgement!

The *Cushing's* jib boom had penetrated one of the *Metis'* watertight compartments. Tons of water poured in, filling her hold and extinguishing the boilers. She sank almost immediately.

Passengers Left
Only four life boats were launched. Captain Burton, A.S. Gallup, director of the steamship line, and members of the crew filled two of the life boats.

Bodies and cargo

washed ashore for days. More than fifty of the one hundred and fifty passengers and crew drowned. Captain Burton lost his license.

Diving The *Metis*
Wreck diver, Captain Bill Palmer provided the following information but not the loran numbers. All semblance of the 200-foot-long *Metis'* wood has disintegrated. On the port and starboard sides are remnants of the copper sheathing that covered the hull.

The boiler, approximately 12 feet in diameter and 20 feet long, is sitting upright. There are scattered pieces of 3-foot-long ceramic pipe which were part of the cargo. Only small pieces of wood remain in front of the boiler.

Protruding from the 20 to 25-foot-high steam engine is a large flywheel and 75-foot-long drive shaft, supported by bearing blocks, with a steel propeller, approximately 15 feet in diameter, at the end.

What artifacts remain are buried under the sand.

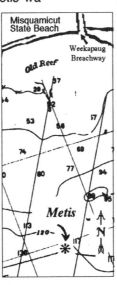

43

Spanish Brig Sunk At Brenton Reef

By Bob Cembrola

- *Minerva*
- Full-rigged wooden brig
  Two masts, square-rigged
  Cast iron swivel guns
  & cannons
- Chart # 13223
  Brenton Point
  .4 NM southwest
  14404.71
  43981.39

Liquor Not Gold

A Spanish wreck in Rhode Island waters? Before you start having Mel Fisher dreams of a cold water *Atocha*, the *Minerva* was a brig not a galleon and was carrying mostly liquor not gold and silver.

Christmas Eve Tragedy

It was Christmas Eve, December 24, 1810. A blinding snowstorm was raging. The reveling Newporters ignored the *Minerva's* distress cannon fire, believing it to be the celebrating crew of an approaching New York packet ship.

The *Newport Mercury* of December 28, 1810 reported the tragedy: "The Spanish brig *Minerva*, 16 days from Havana, bound to Bristol, went ashore on Monday evening last about 7 o'clock on Brenton's reef near the entrance to this harbour, and in a few hours went to pieces. The Supercargo, Captain, mate and seven men were washed from the quarterdeck of the brig, on which they were endeavouring to reach the shore, and drowned. The remainder of the crew, consisting of the boatswain and nine men, succeeded in reaching the shore on pieces of the wreck. The cargo of the *Minerva* consisted of Rum, Wine, Rice and 30 casks Powder, which will be nearly all lost."

Never again was a cannon fired in Rhode Island waters unless a ship was in distress.

Vessel Stripped

The loss of a ship on Brenton Reef was an unfortunately common event as was "wrecking".

This is the stripping of a vessel run aground or otherwise disabled, often times before the entire crew was on shore.

As is usually the case with wooden ships sunk in shallow water on a rocky bottom, she was smashed to pieces while heavier items such as cannon and anchors were dropped to the seabed.

Minerva Discovered

The location of the Minerva and the following information was graciously provided to Marlene and Don Snyder for this book by their friend John Jagschitz, a retired University of Rhode Island Professor, scuba diver, and member of the All American Spearfishing Team.

Divers of the Newport Underwater Sportsmen Club while spearfishing on Brenton Reef off Newport in 1965 sighted cannons under the water. Several cannons were retrieved by Club divers led by John Jagschitz in 1965, 1970, 1971, and by Jim Jenney in 1970.

The identification of the cannons by Jenney, as being part of the armament of the Minerva, was greatly assisted by the discovery at the site by Tom Chilcott of a piece of eight dated 1810. The piece of eight, a Spanish reale,

which had been cast in Colonial Mexico, was cemented to a cluster of cannon balls and musket balls.

Markings on the cannons, the Spanish reale, and his research convinced Jenny that the Minerva had been found.

The Club members were successful in keeping the specifics of the wreck site a secret for almost 30 years.

Diving the Minerva

The shallow depth, 20 feet or less, tide rips, and swells make diving on Brenton Reef dangerous. **Dive only in calm weather at slack tide.**

There are still several sizes of cannon to be seen on the west side of the reef hidden in kelp in 15-25 feet of water.

The remains of the wooden fishing steamer George W. Humphreys, described in another chapter of this book, is also at this site.

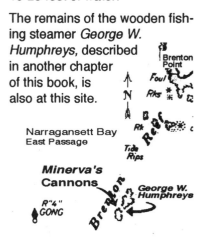

Monhegan Wreck Discovered

by Albert Langner

- *Monhegan*
  Wooden ferry boat

  Length 128 feet
- Prudence Island
  Sandy Point—150 yards north
- Chart # 13223

The Quest

I read about a shipwreck off Prudence Island in the summer of 1994.

My partner and I discovered the wreck on our first excursion to the site. During that visit I uncovered several beautifully embossed registered spring water bottles from companies in Maine.

Monhegan Swallowed Up

The year was 1903 when the mighty *Monhegan* slid into the waters off the Cobb-Butler yard in Portland, Maine.

Measuring 128 feet in length and powered by a triple expansion steam-engine-driven propeller, she proudly graced the waters as Captain I. E. Archibald's new flagship, carrying passengers and freight along the Maine coast.

In 1906 she was swallowed up by the expanding Eastern Steamship Company where, in the summer, she shared the popular Portland, Maine to Rockland, Maine route with the *Mineola.*

It was during this point in time that the bottles I later uncovered were discarded somewhere in the hull. Lost and forgotten in time, they now serve to keep the *Monhegan's* illustrious history alive for future generations.

Proud Flagship Falls Victim

As the 1920's approached, the invasion of cars, trucks, and trains led to the demise of the steamboat business. The *Monhegan* fell victim to these new modes of transportation. In 1919 the Blackstone Valley

Transportation Company of Pawtucket, R.I. purchased the *Monhegan* but kept her for only a short time. The following year the Providence, Fall River and Newport Steamship Company became her new owners. From her home port in Providence, Rhode Island she would make the Block Island, Rhode Island run with a stop over at Newport, Rhode Island.

Disaster Strikes

After 3 1/2 decades of service, disaster struck. On September 21, 1938, Mother Nature served up the worst hurricane the New England coast had ever seen.

Providence took the brunt of the storm's fury leaving the city district buried beneath 7 feet of water. The *Monhegan*, tied at her slip on Dyer Street, proved no match against the hurricane's destructive forces. The storm claimed another victim as the *Monhegan* slipped beneath the surface and sank at her dock.

Cast Off And Abandoned

After the hurricane, service between Providence and Block Island never resumed. The once proud *Monhegan* was refloated, sold to the Interstate Navigation Company and towed to Newport, Rhode Island. In the spring of 1939 the future of the *Monhegan* took a turn for the

worse. A new company bought her and developed big plans to convert her into a floating restaurant off Warwick's Rocky Point Amusement Park.

As the big plans faded and tarnished so did the shiny brass that once decorated the steamboat. It wasn't long before the *Monhegan* was cast off and abandoned on the shores of Prudence Island, Rhode Island where she eventually broke apart and became buried in the sands of Narragansett Bay.

Diving the *Monhegan*

The remains of the *Monhegan* are on the east side of Prudence Island, 150 yards north of the Sandy Point lighthouse close to shore in 5 feet of water.

Dive on the south side of the 1st dock from the point, as the wreck lies underneath it.

Most of what's left of the wreck is concealed by sand. The outline of the wooden hull is visible and following it south toward the bow, you'll spot a pair of bollards lying off the port side.

You'll also encounter cable from the side railings and clumps of orange concretion hiding what's left of some iron fastenings.

47

Diving Watch Hill Reefs &

By Marlene & Don Snyder

Napatree Point

There is no road to the end of the point—you either walk the mile or go by boat. Either way, the trip is worth it. At the far end of Napatree Point are the remains of Fort Mansfield, built in 1898 to protect the coast from enemy warships during the Spanish-American War.

The reefs arch for 3 nautical miles east from the lighthouse at Watch Hill Point to the East Point of Connecticut's Fishers Island. The major reefs from west to east are: Watch Hill Reef, Sugar Reef, and Catumb Rocks.

> **Watch Hill Reefs**
> Chart # 13214

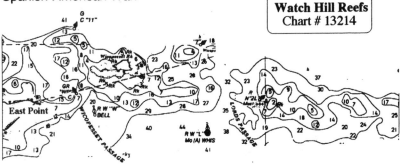

Diving or snorkeling at the far end of the point off the rocky shore near the remains of Fort Mansfield is most rewarding, with visibility averaging 20-40 feet. Legal sized stripers, tautog, and tropical fish make the trip worth it.

Watch Hill Reefs

The Watch Hill Reefs at Rhode Island's western-most border provide the *experienced* diver with some of the most interesting, challenging, and dangerous diving on the east coast.

The reefs rise like jagged mountains 130 feet from the floor of Block Island Sound protruding through or lurking under the surface.

The **current throughout the reef expanse is hazardous at all times**.

Getting to the Reefs

The remains of hundreds of ships decorate the ocean bottom around these reefs: to avoid joining them, venture to the reefs with an experienced captain and crew.

Napatree Point

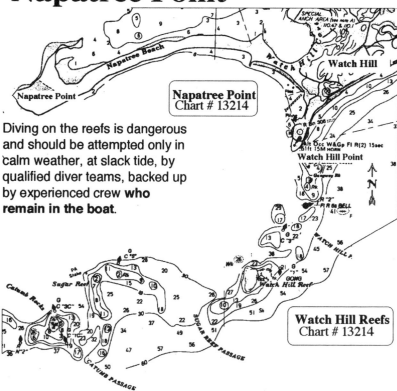

Napatree Point
Chart # 13214

Diving on the reefs is dangerous
and should be attempted only in
calm weather, at slack tide, by
qualified diver teams, backed up
by experienced crew **who
remain in the boat**.

Watch Hill Reefs
Chart # 13214

Diving the Reefs

Why take the chance if diving
here is dangerous? Jim Jenny,
author, marine historian, and
master wreck diver said it best:
"Watch Hill is one of the most
unusual areas in the entire
state."

Depths around the reefs are between 15 and 50 feet. The water
is usually very clear with visibility often exceeding 20 feet. On
bright days sunlight is reflected
off the sandy bottom, further increasing visibility.

The spearfishing is excellent.
This far out you could bag a
record breaking striper.

*Shipwrecks on The Shores of
Westerly* by Margaret Carter,
1973, lists over 200 wrecks on
or near the Watch Hill reefs.

The steel freighter *Onondaga*
sank here on June 18, 1918
when her captain mistook the
Watch Hill light for the lighthouse at Race Rock and sank
her in 35 feet of water on the
northeast side of Watch Hill
reef.

Huge, And Dark, And Sinister

by Marlene & Don Snyder

Pavilion   North Beach Clubhouse   Cabana

- **Container Barge**
- Steel Automobile Carrier
- Narragansett
  North Town Beach
  100 yards off-shore
- Chart # 13223
- 14440.76
  43986.54

Automobile Barge

From The Edge Of Eternity

It is a formidable spectacle. As though something huge, and dark, and sinister has emerged from the deep, or come from the edge of eternity to lie in wait just 100 yards off the Narragansett shore.

Standing on the porch of the Town of Narragansett's North Beach Clubhouse, the enormous proportions of the leviathan can be seen just below the surface of the ocean.

It appears to be slowly inhaling and exhaling, as huge circles of water undulate from the blowholes on its back.

Bow North to the beach, the 40-foot wide, 320-foot long, 10-foot deep specter taunts the diver to enter the belly of the beast.

A Call For Help

It was December 31, 1982, New Year's Eve. The crew of the tug had hoped to celebrate the new year in Newport.

The tug and the mammoth, rusting barge in tow were owned by the Connecticut-based Witte Heavy Lift Salvage Company. The barge was being hauled to Newport's Coddington Cove.

The tug's five man crew first became aware that the barge was taking on water when they were off Block Island. It became obvious to the crew that the water pouring into the hold of the 128,000-cubic-foot barge would soon sink it in 105 feet of water unless they got help.

Coast Guard To The Rescue

The captain of the tug radioed

the Coast Guard. Both the Point Judith and the Newport Coast Guard stations dispatched 41-foot boats and a helicopter to the scene with pumps.

After 90 minutes of pumping, the tug made for the Narragansett shore.

At approximately 11 a.m. the tug and barge reached the Narragansett Town Beach where the barge was grounded in the shallow water, just off-shore. Tug and crew left immediately for Newport, to celebrate no doubt.

Efforts To Remove Barge Fail
No reason for the sinking of the barge was ever found. The Town of Narragansett has been unable to force the now bankrupt former owners or the State of Rhode Island to remove the barge.

Diving Restrictions
1-Between Labor Day and Memorial Day access to the barge from the beach or by boat may be had at any time.

2-Between Memorial Day and Labor Day the barge may be dived only after 6 p.m.

3-Dive the barge only when the sea is flat-calm and there is no surge.

4-At low tide, a person standing on parts of the deck will be out of the water. Take care if coming by boat.

Diving The Barge
The bow of the barge points North. It rises approximately 6 feet off the sand in about twelve feet of water. The sides of the barge are intact. The stern rises about 1 foot from the sand in approximately 20 feet of water.

The interior of the barge can be accessed through deteriorating deck plates. Look for large openings in the deck that can be penetrated without danger of snagging diving gear or injuring yourself. **Important! If there appears to be *any danger* of injury—*don't dive.***

The interior is a labyrinth of steel beams and columns spaced far enough apart to swim through without danger of injury. There are large open areas, 10 feet high and 20-40 feet in length and width, with enough light coming through deck holes to provide excellent visibility.

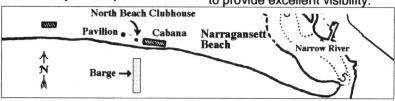

Anti Aircraft Training Center

by Mark Bennett

- **Price Neck**
  Newport—Ocean Drive
- Chart # 13223

Antiaircraft Training Center

Price Neck is located just east of King's Beach in Newport.

In 1942 the U.S. Navy constructed the *Anti Aircraft Training Center At Price Neck* to train antiaircraft gunnery personnel. The area was bustling with activity until the end of World War II.

In November of 1943 alone, the Naval Anti Aircraft Training Center prepared 14,000 enlisted men and 1,000 officers for action in the war. The main gun emplacement still exists as a cement rectangle that crosses the width of Price Neck, from East Cove to West Cove.

The military memorabilia found here is testimony to the sacrifices made by our ancestors so that we might live free.

World War II Artifacts

The shallow clear waters surrounding Price Neck are rich in World War II era military artifacts, including brass shell casings and other hardware. Only feet off the west end of the gun emplacement (which can be seen from King's Beach) rest hundreds of spent rounds of ammunition from .30 caliber machine guns to larger 40mm and 3" guns.

Outstanding Spearfishing

The rocky ocean side of Price Neck protrudes into the Atlantic, making it a favored location for spearfishing.

Tautog and stripers are plentiful here, as this area receives much less fishing pressure than more popular areas. On the east side of Price Neck, fluke and flounder flourish in the cove.

Diving The East Cove
Price Neck's East Cove is protected from nearly all directions, and makes a perfect second dive or alternate dive location.

The transparent shoal makes this an ideal location for snorkeling and for new divers.

Divers can access the east side of Price Neck by kayak or small boat from the Greenbridge boat ramp.

Heading straight out from the boat ramp toward the east end of the gun emplacement, one can see a loading dock (much of which has been recently rebuilt) and the remains of a small dry dock behind a small rock island.

East Cove Navy Anchor
In the middle of the east cove, in fifteen to twenty feet of water, is a huge Navy anchor left by the inhabitants of the training center.

The shank is nearly ten feet long, with flukes extending six feet from tip to tip.

The anchor, the excellent visibility produced by the crystalline water, and the sandy bottom, create an interesting photographic opportunity.

Diving The West Side
The west side of Price Neck is best accessed from King's Beach by kayak, small boat (if the ramp is ever repaired) or a lengthy surface swim.

The ocean side and west end of Price Neck are open to the ocean, so caution should be used if the water is rough.

While there may be surges in the less protected areas around Price Neck, there is no current, so a dive can be made with no regard to the tide.

Rose Island

by Albert Langner

- **Rose Island**
- Narragansett Bay
  East Passage
- Chart # 13223

British Occupation

What Rose Island lacks in size it makes up for in historical significance.

Heading up the east passage, the island is located about a mile west of Newport and just south of the bridge.

History tells us it was the British who first used Rose Island militarily as part of their strategic defense network.

Cannon on Rose Island, in conjunction with those on Goat Island, Brenton's Point, and the mainland were positioned to defend British controlled Newport against an enemy attack from the south.

In 1778 French ships surprised the British with an attack on Newport from the north. Prior to the battle the British abandoned Rose Island, giving our French allies an added advantage.

American troops quickly took over the Island and dug out a small square earthen fort.

Rose Island Forts

War was taking its toll on the British and by 1780 they left Newport entirely. The French came to our aid again as troops under General Rochambeau, assisted by the Rhode Island militia, constructed a large fortification on Rose Island. Armed with 50 cannon, the fort was capable of fending off an attack from the south as well as from the north. At the close of the Revolutionary War the French turned the fort over to American forces. Our new government decided it would be wise to bolster Newport's defenses to ward off any threat from European invaders. Plans were drafted for Fort Hamilton to be built on Rose Island with 60 cannon and barracks for 300 men. Construction got under way but was never finished as the threat of an invasion gradually dwindled.

First Lighthouse

The old fort remained idle until 1869 when Rose Island's first lighthouse was built on part of the existing fortifications. A few years later the Navy moved in and took over the island making it a storage facility for guns, cotton, and explosives.

Later, during WWI and WWII, the barracks and fort became a storehouse for mines, torpedoes and high explosives. Where cannons once stood, antiaircraft guns and 50 caliber machine guns were put in place. After WWII the navy pulled out and the island has remained virtually untouched since.

Diving Rose Island

Rose Island is an excellent dive site for the recreational diver. It's a short boat ride from either the ramp at Fort Adams in Newport or from one of the launches in Jamestown. You'll find the best diving off the south shore.

For sightseeing or lobster hunting, follow the line of rocks that extends out from the south east corner. The maximum depth here is 25-30 feet and is an ideal spot for a night dive.

Wreck Divers

Wreck divers may want to explore what's left of the *Extra,* located just west of these rocks and about 100 feet from shore. Wooden beams and clumps of iron can be found. Following the trail of debris in towards shore, divers report finding small brass objects and bits of wood in and amongst the rocks.

If you're hunting for dinner, you'll find flounder along the flat bottom west of the rocky point. Past the gently sloping sandy bottom, you'll encounter eel grass and then a mud bottom as you get into deeper water.

There is minimal current along the south side and visibility is generally good. Diving off the lighthouse offers different challenges. Shallow water and a rock ledge means lots of surge when the wind is blowing up the bay.

The advanced diver may find an interesting dive off the east side. The bottom drops off sharply to about 110 feet and when the tide is running you'll have current with which to deal. Plan your dive carefully and enjoy the great diving around historic Rose Island.

Solitude And The Sea

by Marlene & Don Snyder

- **Sakonnet Point**
  Southern-most point
- Chart # 13221

A Unique Experience

There are few places in Rhode Island that offer as much to those who love solitude and the sea as does the Tiverton-Little Compton peninsula. Walking, fishing, boating, lobstering, snorkeling, scuba diving, spearfishing, wine tasting or just relaxing by the sea—it is all there and more.

The peninsula forms Rhode Island's eastern-most terminus. It is bounded on the west by the Sakonnet River, on the east by the Massachusetts border, and on the south by Rhode Island Sound.

Sakonnet Point Breakwater

To reach the breakwater that forms the entrance to Sakonnet Harbor, follow State Highway 77, West Main Road, which branches right in Sakonnet and becomes Sakonnet Point Road. From Sakonnet Point Road, turn right on Bluffhead Road and follow it to where it ends at the breakwater. On-site parking is available at the breakwater, but there is no public boat ramp.

The breakwater is an ideal location to spend a summer day . The views are spectacular. Water craft of every variety ply the Sakonnet River. The Sakonnet Yacht club is home port to pleasure craft that are continually going to or returning from Rhode Island Sound.

Diving the Breakwater

Subsurface visibility in this location is often in excess of 20 feet due to several factors. The Sakonnet River, the East Passage and the West Passage are Narragansett Bay's three en-

56

trances and exits. However, the Sakonnet waterway is almost free of the volume of commercial/domestic drainage which often adversely affects the East and West Passages.

Depths outside the breakwater descend gradually to 24 feet. On the inside, the water is only eight feet deep.

Diving and snorkeling at the breakwater are excellent. Spear-fishing for tautog is often rewarded with a great catch. Many lobsters are also taken at the breakwater.

The Offshore Islands
You will need a boat to reach the offshore Islands. There is a boat ramp at Sakonnet Harbor Fishing Access. The Access is located at the southern end of State Route 77, the Sakonnet Point Road. The single-width concrete boat ramp crosses a beach into Sakonnet Harbor, a sheltered basin which accesses the Sakonnet River directly to Rhode Island Sound. Across the road from the boat ramp is a 48-hour parking area for trailers and cars.

Launch your boat, and head south on the Sakonnet River past the abandoned lighthouse to the West and East Islands approximately 1/2 nautical mile from the ramp. **Exercise Extreme Caution**: the rocks in the area you are about to enter rise nearly to the surface.

West and East Islands rise up from Schuyler Ledge. The ledge protrudes from Sakonnet Point for a nautical mile south into Rhode Island Sound.

West Island
West Island's Sakonnet River side, the west side, is a unique diving location. The island's sheer cliffs plunge precipitously to the water's shimmering surface and continue to the ocean floor 20 to 30 feet below.

The sandy bottom, clear water, forests of eel grass rising nearly to the surface, and varieties of tropical and native fish make diving here superb.

East Island
East Island with its mysterious rock columns is surrounded by shallow water best left to kayaks, small boats and snorkeling. It is a great place for a picnic and exploring.

57

The Death Of *Samson*

by Marlene & Don Snyder with Dive Master Steven J. Dumas

- *Samson*
- Steel Barge
  Length 140 feet, Beam 40 feet
  Heigth 10 feet
- Chart # 13219
- Point Judith Harbor of Refuge
  Middle Breakwater

Barge Cut In Half

The spud barge *Samson* was owned by the Harbor Marine Company, Warren, Rhode Island. It had been purchased in Maine by Harbor Marine to work on the Jamestown-Verrazzano Bridge which opened in 1992.

The *Samson* had originally been a 300-foot-long, 40-foot-wide, 10-foot-high barge used for transporting railroad cars.

The *Samson* was converted to a construction barge by being cut in half. A 70-foot-high A-frame crane, powered by a 671 Detroit diesel engine, with a lifting capacity of 300 tons was installed on the stern. Two steel spuds, 40 feet long, 18" in diameter with pointed ends which were driven into the ocean floor to stabilize the barge when it was working, were added. A small,

steel-tracked creeper coring crane used to raise and lower the spuds and to move equipment was on the deck when the *Samson* sank.

The Detroit diesel engine also powered a 2-drum waterfall-type winch which controlled the anchors.

The barge had a pneumatic winch welded on the deck which was used for various pulling operations and for moving the barge back and forth on anchors.

The barge had wood chafing on three sides.

Hurricane Service

Hurricane Bob ravaged the Rhode Island Coast in September 1991.

On October 4, 1991 the *Samson*

58

was towed to Point Judith Harbor of Refuge to raise a Coast Guard signal light which the hurricane had toppled from the point of the east breakwater.

Samson Rolls On Side

Carelessly anchored that night inside the middle breakwater with no pumps operating, the leaky old barge began to fill with water.

At 7:30 a.m., October 5, 1991, the barge, half-filled with water, rolled over on its starboard side.

The end of the crane's 70-foot-long A-frame hit the bottom and kept the barge from turning completely over.

The *Samson* remained half submerged with the port side above the waterline for several weeks.

Samson Turns Turtle

Storms and wave action eventually broke the A-frame loose from the barge. The barge turned turtle and submerged in 30-35 feet of water,15 feet below the water line at its highest point.

Finding The *Samson*

From the tip of the middle breakwater's east opening, the *Samson* is 300-400 yards southwest, next to the wall. The bow, rake, is approximately 40 feet from the wall. The barge is in a north-south position.

Diving The *Samson*

The protected location of the *Samson*, just inside the Point Judith Harbor of Refuge's middle breakwater, in 30-35 feet of water, make it an excellent stormy weather or second, shallow water dive site.

The *Samson* is upside down, bow to the center breakwater. The A-frame is broken off the barge and lays partially buried in the mud in an east west direction.

The coring crane is under the *Samson* and has punched a hole through the deck of the barge. The tank-like steel treads of the crane and parts of the engine are clearly visible under the hull.

The coring crane's boom is broken off and extends from the wreck toward the Middle Breakwater wall.

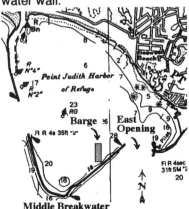

A Plane for all Seasons

by George A. Flynn,
Article & Graphics

- **Skyraider**
- Charlestown
  Breachway, south
  Depth 25-30 feet
  14529.5
  43969.6

Author's Note: Lawrence D. Webster, an aircraft archeologist, provided technical information for this article.

Hunter Killer

The prop-driven Douglas Skyraider had served the Navy well. From the time it was introduced into the Navy's air arsenal in the late 40's, through the Korean War, and into the late 60's, the Skyraider had been cast in a wide variety of roles.

With a Hunter Killer designation, it had bombing, strafing and mine-laying capabilities. At Quonset Point Navel Air Station, the Skyraider's mission was Night and All Weather Attack, Pathfinding, Radar Countermeasures and Special Weapons Delivery (nuclear).

Heroism and Tragedy

On the Morning of December 27, 1957, an AD-5W Skyraider, with a crew of 3, was performing routine training drills of "touch and go" landings at Charlestown

Auxiliary field when the pilot noticed smoke coming from the engine. From their present altitude of 1,000 feet, he managed to climb to 1,500 feet for a little more "elbow room".

He instructed the crew to make the necessary ditching preparations and turned the plane back to the field for an emergency landing.

Flames were now coming from the engine, and it was rapidly losing power—it would be impossible to reach the field. Seconds later, with all power gone, the Skyraider with its heavy load of radar and electronic equipment, dropped like a stone, hit the water hard, and sank almost immediately.

Rescue Helicopters

Two rescue helicopters were on the scene within minutes of the crash where they found the life-jacketed crew afloat in the frigid water. The pilot and crew chief were able to hang onto a sling that had been lowered by a helicopter and were towed to shore. The third crew member, either dazed or unconscious, had been unable to grab the sling and died of injuries or exposure to the icy water. The Navy made no attempt to salvage the plane. It was not marked on the charts.

Diver Finds Skyraider
In the case of the Skyraider, a local diver, Ray Rathbone, found the plane while he was spearfishing in 1960. Rathbone told the author during a January 1995 telephone conversation that the plane, still fairly intact,

was lying belly-up amidst a rocky, overgrown area with the wings attached and one wheel pointing toward the surface. By all appearances, the angle of entry and the weight of the engine, combined with forward motion of the plane, had caused it to cartwheel while sinking. Rathbone removed a serial number which later helped to identify the plane from records kept at Quonset Point.

Diving The Skyraider
Captain Bill Roe dove the Skyraider numerous times in recent years and reports it to be in sad shape. The engine has separated from the fuselage and is lying 25 feet away in the sand. Captain Roe says, "There really isn't much to see. From a distance, you are not going to see it as a plane. It's not an easy wreck to find. A lot of the time, I use land points and then go down and do circles. Sometimes, I'm right on it. Other times, it takes a half hour to find."

Spartan Wrecked On Block Island

by John Stanford

- *Spartan*
  Steel freighter
  Length 222 feet 5 inches
  Beam 37 feet 9 inches
  Depth 16 feet 5 inches
  Gross tonnage 1,596
- Block Island
  Old Harbor Point, south
- Chart # 13217
  14531.21
  43877.55

SPARTAN WRECKED ON BLOCK ISLAND.

Local Freight Steamer Has 15-Foot Hole in Bow and is in Danger of Complete Destruction from Heavy Sea.—Part of Crew Taken Off.

Such was the headline that greeted readers of the March 20, 1905 edition of the *Providence Daily Journal*.

The Steamer *Spartan* was just one of many vessels to become ensnared on the shallow rocky reef and shoals surrounding Block Island.

Fall River To Philadelphia
The *Spartan* was built in Wilmington, Delaware in 1883 for the Philadelphia Steamship Company. She was used by the Winsor Line to ship manufactured goods including textiles from the mills in Fall River to Philadelphia.

Groping In The Fog
On the day she was lost, she was under the command of Captain J. O'Connell Briggs of East Providence, Rhode Island and had a crew of 22 men.

The *Spartan* was bound from Providence, Rhode Island for Philadelphia, Pennsylvania. She made a slow run down Narragansett Bay, passed Beavertail Point and was headed for Block Island when a thick fog set in.

Unfortunately for the crew, they had altered course to the westward before they had cleared Block Island's southeastern coast. Visibility was zero.

Fate Had Other Plans

Fate had other plans for the good ship. The crew was horrified as the *Spartan* fetched up on a reef off Green Hill Point at 4:15 a.m. on March 19, 1905. Because she ran aground in shallow water, the off-loading of cargo started as soon as the seas were calm.

It was at first thought that the *Spartan* could be saved by building a false bottom to cover the 15 foot gash in her hull. She would then be pumped out and refloated.

All efforts to save the wounded ship were frustrated by the following conditions: the tide was high when she struck, the *Spartan* was impaled hard and fast on the rocks, and for days after the mishap large storm swells pounded the vessel in her rocky bed and at times broke completely over her.

Calico Hill

As the vessel was slowly being pounded on the shore of Block Island, the salvagers were working steadily to remove the cargo of miscellaneous goods, including cotton cloth, rubber goods, print goods, etc. Many enterprising islanders acquired portions of the saltwater-soaked bolts of cloth.

The natives spread so much of the fabric to dry on a hill above Old Harbor that even today this island landmark is known as Calico Hill. Less than a year after the grounding, the seas had broken the vessel so thoroughly that nothing remained above the waves.

Diving the *Spartan*

Today the remains of the *Spartan* can be found a short way south of Old Harbor Point. She lies in 14 feet of water on the North side of a rocky reef that extends to shore. After 89 years on the bottom there isn't much left of the ship. The site is great for a second dive or snorkeling.

Lying on their sides are two boilers approximately 10 feet in diameter and 15 feet long. The fire tubes are still in the boilers.

A person standing on top of one of the boilers at low tide will be out of the water. Scattered throughout the site, divers will see steel plates, beams, control wheels, and a large cargo hatch covering.

Two Cautions

Dive here only when the ocean is calm. Large swells can make diving very hazardous.

Also be very careful when operating a boat in the area. There are several large boulders which lie just under the surface.

The Sea Claims Another Prize

by Bob Cembrola

- ***P.T. Teti***
  Steel tugboat
- Newport Neck
  Brenton Point
  8 NM south
- Chart #
  14382.5
  43930.96

  Graphic by
  Marlene Snyder
  from a slide by
  Brian Skerry

NOS—Mystery Tug

In November 1992 the U.S. Department of Commerce's, National Oceanic and Atmospheric Administration (NOAA), National Ocean Service (NOS) issued the following Automated Wreck and Obstruction Information System(AWOIS) report:

"While searching for AWOIS 6949 (a fishing vessel later determined to be nonexistent) (34 FT F/V) side scan sonar detected an unknown tugboat approximately 60-80 feet in length, lying in NE SW orientation.

The Tug is in one piece and rests upright on her keel in 90 ft of water. Divers determined the shoalest point to be the stack. Least Depth on the wreck was 24.1 meters—79 ft. (11/92)".

Hours of Sleuthing

Editors Note: Hours of sleuthing, research, and countless telephone calls by the author of this article, Bob Cembrola, uncovered the following information about the unknown AWOIS Tug.

The *Chemung*

She was named the *Chemung*. The *Chemung* was a steel-hulled canal tug built by the Ira Bushey Shipyard, Brooklyn, New York and launched in September 1937.

She is 85 feet long, with a 19 foot beam, and a 9 foot draft. Her folding mast and low-profile pilot house and smokestack enabled her to pass under low canal trestles and bridges.

The *Chemung* spent the first twenty years or so of her life with a dredging company in New York City which had her hauling dredge spoils in the New York State Barge Canal. She was then sold to the New England Dredge & Dock Company in New Haven, Connecticut.

From *Chemung* To *P.T. Teti*

Her new owner, Harold Teti, renamed her *P.T. Teti* and converted her from steam to a Fairbanks diesel with 575 horsepower fed to a single screw. After being converted from steam to diesel, the *P.T. Teti* worked in mostly towing situations until she was sold to a Rhode Island company engaged in the same type of work.

Sea Claims Another Prize

Ironically, in 1972 while under tow herself from Fairhaven, Massachusetts to Point Judith, Rhode Island, she began taking on water in heavy seas and capsized. Her cable was cut, allowing the sea to claim another prize.

Other Tugs Lost Nearby

While the exact cause of sinking may never be known or perhaps revealed, this particular wreck is not associated with loss of life, a famous battle or unusual marine architecture. Rumor has it that a couple of other tugs have been lost nearby, mysteriously sinking in a deep hole. A coincidence?

Diving the *Teti*

Fortunately for divers, the *P.T. Teti* now rests essentially upright on a sand bottom in 100 feet of water. She has been fairly well stripped of easily removable items; only her prop remains for the enterprising and determined bronze hound.

The attraction here is the hull and surrounding environment. As her hatches are wide open, penetration is easy and relatively safe, a good practice spot especially with the generally decent visibility often exceeding 35 feet.

The *Teti* is almost totally covered with anemones and is frequented by various species of fish, some of whom are quite friendly.

The *Teti* is not for those in search of souvenirs; the only thing you're likely to return with is the memory of an interesting dive and maybe a big lobster.

Exercise Extreme Caution

The *Teti* is within 2 Nautical miles of the *Buzzards Bay Outbound Traffic Lane.* Large commercial vessels straying from the traffic lane may not be able to stop, even if they see your dive boat.

Be prepared to retrieve your divers, have your crew *haul anchor* and get underway fast!

Unraveling The Mystery

by Marlene & Don Snyder

- **Unknown boat**
- Misquamicut
  2.7 NM south
  Chart # 13215
- 14593.5
  43953.9

Shipwreck Research

We may never know for sure the name or history of the shipwreck that we discover. Nevertheless, intellectual honesty demands that we exercise every effort to unravel the mystery.

In understanding what we are seeing, we experience emotionally the significance of the death and entombment of a vessel and perhaps its occupants.

Those of us who dive and write about diving in Rhode Island waters are indebted to those who proceeded us. They did the original research, and diving, and writing.

What Is Research?

You are doing it now. Research means going to every source possible to find the answers. Those sources include books,

divers, fishermen, boat captains, nautical charts, newspapers, etc.

In Rhode Island, the Providence Journal is an outstanding source of information.

The Providence Library's, Rhode Island Collection cross-references *Providence Journal* and *Providence Evening Bulletin* shipwreck articles back to 1820.

The researcher can go to the microfilm files to read, and for a fee, obtain hard copies of the original articles.

Research For This Book

That is how much of the research for the original *Rhode Island Adventure Diving* and this volume, *Rhode Island Adventure Diving II,* was done.

The *Hercules*?
In his 1987 book, *Scuba Northeast,* author Bob Bachand called the Unknown boat the tug *Hercules.*

In 1989 Tim Coleman and Charley Soares, the authors of *Fishable Wrecks & Rockpiles,* wrote that according to a local newspaper of the day, the *Hercules* had sunk just off the Misquamicut State Beach not 2 NM south as Bachand had written.

The authors of this book researched and found a December 14,1907 *Newport Mercury* newspaper article which described the sinking of the *Hercules* 1,000 feet off the Misquamicut State Beach as Coleman and Soars had indicated. Captain Bill Palmer told the authors how to find the wreck. After diving on the *Hercules*, the authors wrote the article that appears elsewhere in this book.

The *William Maloney*?
Coleman and Soares wrote that marine historian Jim Jenny had speculated that the Unknown was a tug named the *William Maloney.*

The *Maloney* and her crew mysteriously disappeared on a trip from Brooklyn, New York to Newport, Rhode Island in November 1924.

So What Is Out There?
All we really know is that the Unknown is not the *Hercules.* As Coleman and Soars wrote: "Time and more research will tell."

Diving the Unknown
The following description of the remains of the Unknown were provided to the authors of this article in March 1995 by Captain Wayne Gordon, an experienced charter boat operator and scuba diver.

What little remains of the vessel rises 4 feet or so off the ocean floor in 95 feet of water.

The Unknown had a wood hull and appears to have been approximately 40 feet in length.

Ten feet or so of the bow and its recessed deck remain. The gunnel rises about four feet to the bow which still points upward.

The engine block protrudes from the mud behind the bow in a position that would have been midship. It appears that part of the engine was salvaged sometime in the past. There is no drive shaft or prop visible; they may be buried in the mud. It is speculated that a vessel of this size would have had a prop no larger than 2 feet in diameter.

If you discover the identity of the Unknown, please contact us.

Glass Containers In The Bay

by Marlene & Don Snyder

The onion bottle shown here was drawn by Marlene Snyder from a photograph by Mark Bennett. The bottle was discovered under the Goat Island causeway. This type of bottle first appeared in America in the mid-17th century.

Onion Bottle— Mid-17th Century

At The Dawn Of Time
Before there was recorded history there was glass.

At the dawn of time our ancestors made arrowheads, scrapers, and other tools from quartz, agate, and obsidian—all natural forms of glass.

The Egyptians
A thousand years before Christ was born, the Egyptians made containers by winding fine threads of hot glass around sand, or by dipping a sand core into molten glass.

When the glass cooled and hardened, the sand was removed, producing a crude vessel.

The sand method described above was long and tedious, requiring hours of labor to produce each one.

Glass Blowing
Glass blowing was developed sometime between 3000 B.C. and 20 B.C. Compared to the sand method employed by the Egyptians, glass blowing was fast.

Blowing Tube And Gather

The glass blower first dipped a hollow iron tube into a pot of molten glass, lifted out the glob of glass—called a gather—and then blew gently into the free end of the tube.

When the resulting bubble in the middle of the molten glass expanded to the desired thinness and size, the bottle was allowed to cool and harden. It was then broken away from the rod.

First Bottles In America

The first American bottles were made without the use of molds.

Early in the nineteenth century dip molds and pattern dip molds came into use. Instead of free-forming the glass, the blower placed the gather into a form of the desired shape and blew until it filled the mold. The blowpipe was melted away from the bottle by a process called "empontilling" which left a rough pontil mark on the bottom of the bottle.

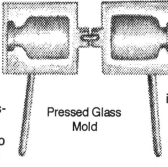

Dip Mold

Around 1825 pressed glass molds, which approximated the size and shape of the finished container, came into use.

The Most Sought After Bottles

Bottles produced before 1905 are those most likely to be of historical significance.

There are certain characteristics to look for when attempting to determine the age of a bottle.

Pressed Glass Mold

Mold Marks

The molds, described above, left seams running up the sides of the bottles. Old free-formed bottles have no mold marks.

Mold marks that run almost to the top of the bottle indicate a machine-made post 1905 bottle.

Bottles produced between 1890 and 1905 usually have mold marks that end an inch below the mouth. Bottles produced before 1880 have mold seams that end low on the neck.

Pontil Marks

The rough pontil marks left by empontilling indicate a bottle made before 1865.

Embossed Lettering may or may not establish the exact age and value of a bottle.

Uneven Glass Thickness

Uneven glass thickness usually indicates that the bottle is old.

Designs

A design which appears on the outside and the inside of a bottle indicates that it is hand-blown.

Bubbles

American bottles with bubbles are without a question old.

Screw Top

Bottles with screw tops on the outside are not old, those with screw tops on the inside are old.

Note: Please turn page.

69

Shapes & Colors

by Marlene & Don Snyder

Evolution Of The Onion Bottle

1650

1660

1680

Evolution Of Onion Bottles
The shapes and colors of bottles may indicate their origin, evolution, age, and use.

As an example of bottle sleuthing and research, the mid-17th century onion bottle used to illustrate the previous article evolved over the next several hundred years from a squatty, dark green colored container to a slender cylindrical shape similar to the wine bottles of today.

The onion bottles original squatty shape was attributable to its hand blown method of manufacture.

The introduction of dip molds and pattern dip molds in the early nineteenth century enabled glass makers to produce bottles of uniform shape.

1770

1800

1830

70

Gin Bottles Or Case Bottles

Case bottles were designed to be packed in wooden crates for shipping. They were blown into square molds.

| 17th Century | 18th Century |

The first case bottles arrived in this country in the 17th century filled with Dutch gin or Jamaican rum. Case bottle production in America began around 1750.

Gin Bottles are easily dated by their form, color, and lip application.

Medicine Bottles

Medicine bottles are among the most widely found of all bottles at wreck sites.

Like onion bottles and case bottles, their size and shapes have changed through time and can provide important clues for dating them and the wreck on which they were found. Refer to the *Monhegan* article in this book for an example of research using bottles found at a wreck.

Evolution Of Medicine Bottles

Early 17th Century

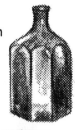

Late 17th Century

Early 18th Century

Late 18th Century

Early 19th Century

Artificial Reefs For Rhode Island?

by William R. Gordon, Jr.

Original Jamestown Bridge 1940-1992

Divers Travel To Rhode Island

Rhode Island is well-known as one of the most popular sport diving destinations on the east coast.

Starting in spring and continuing into late fall, divers travel from many other states to explore the mysteries under the sea at Fort Wetherill and Beavertail in Jamestown, as well as many other excellent dive locations.

The importance of the sport diving industry is recognized as part of the background research being conducted by the Rhode Island Department of Transportation (RIDOT).

The use of the old Jamestown Bridge as a series of artificial reefs in Rhode Island's near and off-shore waters would greatly enhance that industry.

Jamestown Bridge A Reef?

In 1992 the Jamestown–Verrazzano Bridge replaced the original Jamestown Bridge as the principal route from North Kingstown across Narragansett Bay to Jamestown. Constructed in 1940, the Jamestown Bridge has been a familiar landmark for those individuals frequenting the Narragansett Bay area.

Bridge Slated For Demolition

No longer in service, the bridge was slated for demolition and removal. Originally intended for the scrap yard and land fill, the disposal of the tremendous volume of concrete (38,000 cubic yards) and steel materials (27,000 tons) is now being reconsidered in light of the success of man-made underwater reefs in other locations along U.S. coastal waters.

My graduate students and I, as the artificial reef consultant to RIDOT on this project, have been focusing on determining the need for and benefits from deploying the bridge as a series of reefs for various user groups, including sport divers.

Divers And Reefs

Deployed to attract and provide protective habitat for numerous species of fish, artificial reefs have long been popular diving locales in the mid and south Atlantic states, as well as in the Gulf of Mexico. In regard to the needs and interests of the sport diving community, there has been relatively little development of these aquatic structures occurring in New England.

Divers And The Economy

Our research has concluded that recreational diving is a significant element in the tourism economy of Rhode Island. Our preliminary estimates indicate that sport divers contribute somewhere between five and ten million dollars to the Rhode Island economy.

Our surveys of sixteen local dive shops, as well as surveys of resident and non–resident divers at Fort Wetherill and Beavertail revealed a principal interest or need to increase the opportunities for shoreline access and diving. Although under investigation, the necessity for adequate parking and access infrastructure is one of the major concerns in accommodating this need.

Bridges Final Fate?

Although the final fate of the bridge in terms of its use and deployment as artificial reefs remains undetermined at the time this article was written, March 1995, the process underway has demonstrated a greater need to develop and implement a state artificial reef plan and program to address the broader interests and needs of the sport diving community.

Increased recreational opportunities arising from such programs will likely increase tourist revenues, providing economic benefits to Rhode Island's various tourism and marine trade industries.

Brenton Reef Tower Lost

The recent deployment of the Brenton Reef Tower as an artificial reef in another State was considered a major loss of habitat by many marine recreational enthusiasts.

The responsible and careful deployment of the Jamestown Bridge as a series of artificial reefs will represent one of the largest and most significant reef development activities to date on the east coast.

British Warships Burned & Scuttled

by Marlene & Don Snyder

Cerberus
Frigate

Graphic by
Marlene Snyder
From a slide by
Bob Cembrola

British Occupy Newport

In 1778, the British occupiers of Newport intentionally burned and scuttled 10 to 12 of their warships to keep them from being captured by the colonists' French allies.

The charred hulls of those ships, and the personal possessions of the crews remain today where they sank two centuries ago—in the Sakonnet River and close to the shores of Portsmouth and Newport.

Their destruction and discovery 200 years later by a scuba diver is a fascinating story.

The British Invasion

The American War for Independence from Great Britain began on April 19, 1775.

At that time, Newport was one of the largest and most significant ports on the east coast. Unfortunately, privateering, the quasilegal pirating of enemy ships, had become one of Newport's most profitable and acceptable forms of business.

So many sailors were recruited for privateering that Rhode Island was unable to launch a navy to protect Newport from a British invasion. On December 7th, 1776, the British fleet arrogantly sailed up Narragansett Bay's East Passage, into Newport Harbor, and disgorged an army of occupation.

Newport Under Siege

In the spring of 1778, General George Washington devised a brilliant plan to liberate Newport.

A juggernaut of 10,000 Massachusetts and New York soldiers would attack the British army in Newport from the north. Simultaneously, a superior fleet of 16 French vessels would destroy the British fleet and land 2,800 crack marines.

British Terrified
On the morning of July 28, 1778, the British were terrified by the sight of sixteen heavily armed French ships-of-the-line and four frigates sailing up the East Passage with the same impudence the British had shown eighteen months before.

The British intentionally rammed and torched 10-12 of their own warships on the rocky Aquidneck shores in an attempt to keep the French from destroying or capturing them.

Death Of The Warships
Captain Frederick MacKenzie, an Officer of the Regiment of Royal Welsh Fusiliers, witnessed the destruction of some of the British warships on the 5th of August 1778. He wrote in his diary:

"About 5 this morning the two French ships . . . got underway and stood round the N. point of Connonicut, toward The *Cerberus* Frigate, which lay under the W. side of this Island (Aquidneck) nearly opposite the opening between Connonicut

and Prudence. On seeing them in motion, the *Cerberus* slipped her cable and endeavored to get down to town (Newport); but . . . Captain Symmons was obliged to run her ashore behind Redwoods and set her on fire. All the crew got safe ashore. The ship blew up about 8 o'clock.

The *Orpheus, Lark* and *Pigot* Galley, observing the other French ships coming up between Prudence and this Island were immediately run on shore . . . where after the crews had landed, they were set on fire. . .

The Explosion of some of our Frigates was very great, particularly that of The *Lark*, which had 76 barrels of powder in her Magazine. . . ."

Locations of British Wrecks
See the "British Warship Location Charts" article in this book.

French Siege Ends
The French siege of Newport ended nine days later when violent storms forced them to withdraw to Boston for repairs. Washington's 10,000 soldiers retreated when reinforcements failed to appear. The British voluntarily left Newport in October 1779.

The Discovery
The discovery of the British warships in 1973 is described in the following article.

British Warships Found

by Marlene & Don Snyder

The Discovery

In 1973, Albert Davis, Jr., then a graduate student in the Ocean Engineering Department, University of Rhode Island (URI), assisted by faculty members and fellow students, discovered three British frigates: HMS *Orpheus*, *Lark*, and *Cerberus* off the coast of Portsmouth and Newport.

An Obsession

Al's obsession began in 1969 when a friend of the 20-year-old scuba diver told him that the remains of British Revolutionary warships lay just off the shores of Portsmouth, Rhode Island and Newport, Rhode Island.

The archeological study of shipwrecks requires precise recovery techniques. Underwater Bicentennial Expedition, Albert P. Davis, Jr. et al. Department of Ocean Engineering, University of Rhode Island, 1976.

For three years Al searched libraries and museums, and read everything he could get his hands on in an attempt to pinpoint the locations of the wrecks.

The discovery of an old chart with approximate locations of the wrecks proved to be more frustrating than helpful. Nevertheless, weather permitting, Al continued to dive every week-end for three years—and his efforts finally paid off with the discovery of enough evidence to keep him going—a copper barrel hoop, spikes, and cannon balls.

In 1972 his father went to England where he found a wreck-site map at the British Museum and the log of the *Cerberus* at the Greenwich Maritime Museum.

Within two days of his father's

return from England, Al Davis used the map and log to locate the *Cerberus*. For nearly 200 years it had remained undisturbed and hidden in 20 feet of water, just a few yards off the Portsmouth shore.

The ballast heap of the *Cerberus* was surrounded by charred and waterlogged heavy oak planking.

The divers recovered 50 cannonballs with the British broad arrow embossed on them, three cannons, pulley sheaves, a pewter English teapot, the ship's anchor, a section of the ship stove, copper barrel hoops, brandy bottles, wine and rum bottles, hand grenades, lignumvitae pulley sheaves with bronze bushings, leather shoes, sealskin boots, copper coins, ballast bars, and a musket plate datestamped 1746.

Lark and *Orpheus* Discovered
Two weeks after finding the *Cerberus*, Davis found the *Lark's* ballast pile and rotting hull timbers approximately three nautical miles north of the *Cerberus*.

During the winter of 1973 he found the largest of the scuttled British ships, the *Orpheus*, approximately one nautical mile south of the *Lark*. Like the other wrecks, she was surrounded by 3,000 pound cannons.

London Public Records Office documents revealed that "Time did not allow the removal of the crew's hammocks or personal belongings, prior to the ship's destruction. . ."

Unfortunately, time and money ran out before the project really got under way. Today the scattered wreckage of the *Cerberus*, *Lark*, *Orpheus* and *Juno*, three British ships in the Sakonnet River, and at least five other British ships remain where they sank.

The Transport Ships
One of the students assisting Davis was Robert Cembrola.

In 1987, Cembrola discovered the scattered remains of a British troopship scuttled in Newport Harbor in 1778.

In July 1989 the *Rhode Island Maritime Heritage Foundation*, a voluntary group of scuba divers of which Bob Cembrola was a member, revealed that in the fall of 1988, they had discovered the remains of five British transport ships.

The transport ships were just off the Newport shore in 20 to 50 feet of water.

The fascinating story of those transport ships is described by Bob Cembrola in the following article in this book.

British Transport Ships Scuttled

by Bob Cembrola

British Army Of Occupation

During the American Revolutionary War, 1775-1783, England faced the daunting task of supplying her entire army of occupation by ship.

The British occupiers of Newport had great difficulty procuring both food and firewood because the locals remained loyal to the American cause.

18th Century Freighters

The British resorted to foraging missions utilizing transport vessels, the freighters of the 18th century. So great was the need for wood by the British troops in Newport that by the end of 1777, they had cut every usable tree from Aquidneck, Prudence and Jamestown Islands as well as the shores of southern Narragansett Bay.

Transport Ship Specifications

Transport generally referred to the function of a vessel, not a particular hull form or rig. During the Revolution, a ship had to pass a rigorous inspection at a Royal dockyard, usually Deptford, England in order to qualify.

The inspection included: framing, planking, masts, yards and rigging, hull drilling and probing to determine the soundness of the wood, and size: height between decks at least 4'10" and a burden of 200 tons. Shipowners were required to equip their vessels with at least six cannon of six pound shot. All vessels destined for North America were ballasted with coal, providing fuel for soldiers on arrival, a measure which provided very temporary relief from firewood scavenging missions.

The rules were ignored or bent beyond recognition as the situation demanded, thus the nature of remains of the transport ships in Newport Harbor are difficult to predict.

Transports Scuttled

The approaching superior French fleet caused Captain Ralph Brisbaine, commander of British naval forces in Newport, to scuttle virtually the entire British fleet.

The transports were stripped and scuttled to block the French ships of the line from entering Newport Harbor.

Captain Frederick Mackenzie, an Officer of the Regiment of Royal Welsh Fusiliers, who witnessed the scuttling in August 1778 wrote: "several large transports have been sunk off the North Batt. and Goat Island so that no line of Battle ship can bring up nearer to them than 800 yds." These six and five more were scuttled between Goat Island and Rose Island on August 3; four more were placed in the channel on the south side of Goat Island on August 5th. Their masts were cut off leaving enough above water to remain visible to the French com-

manders, hopefully dissuading them from approaching too close to shore. Mackenzie reports on August 8: "the nearest ship anchored about 3 miles from the N. battery. It was conjectured that the sight of the Masts of the ships sunk in front of Goat Island deterred them from bringing up off that Island."

Frigates and Sloops Scuttled

That same day, the British engaged the French with their shore batteries. To keep them from falling into French hands, the British in a final act of desperation burned and sank more of their own vessels: the sloop *Faulcon* off the southeastern end of Goat Island, the frigate *Flora* between Long Wharf and Goat Island, and the *Grand Duke* transport, converted from an East Indiaman, was burnt between Goat Island and the north battery .

Diving Newport Harbor

Shore access is season dependent. During the boating months, try Van Zandt pier or other Washington Street points. Otherwise, any pier along Thames Street will do. When diving by boat, any place you drop your hook has the potential to deliver wrecks and other vestiges.

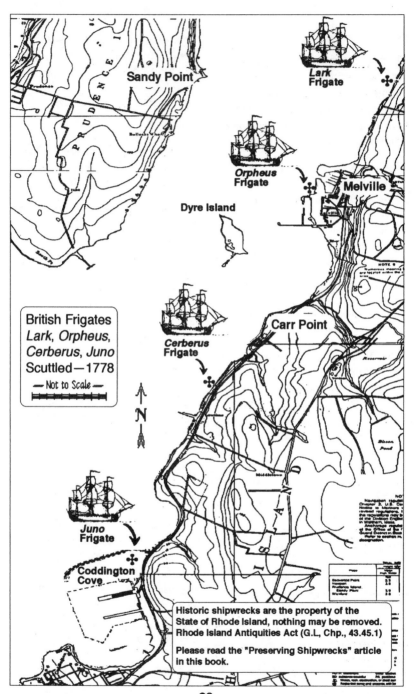

Sandy Point

Lark
Frigate

Orpheus
Frigate

Melville

Dyre Island

Carr Point

Cerberus
Frigate

British Frigates
*Lark, Orpheus,
Cerberus, Juno*
Scuttled—1778

— Not to Scale —

↑
N

Juno
Frigate

Coddington
Cove

Historic shipwrecks are the property of the
State of Rhode Island, nothing may be removed.
Rhode Island Antiquities Act (G.L, Chp., 43.45.1)

Please read the "Preserving Shipwrecks" article
in this book.

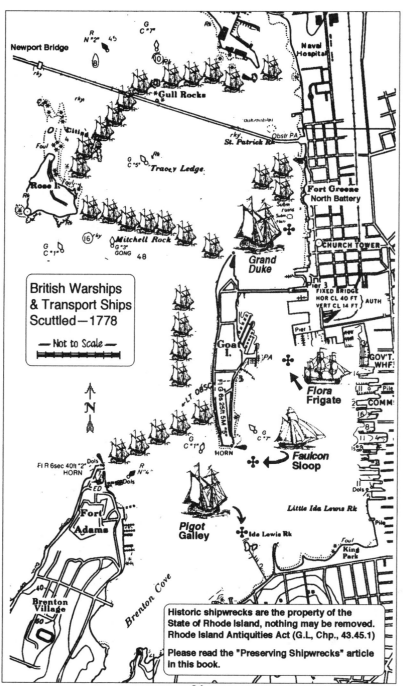

British Warships
& Transport Ships
Scuttled—1778

— Not to Scale —

Grand Duke

Flora Frigate

Faulcon Sloop

Pigot Galley

Fort Adams

Brenton Village

Newport Bridge

Naval Hospital

Gull Rocks

St. Patrick R

Tracey Ledge

Rose I.

Mitchell Rock

Fort Greene North Battery

CHURCH TOWER

FIXED BRIDGE
HOR CL 40 FT
VERT CL 14 FT   AUTH

Goat I.

GOV'T. WHF.

COMM

HORN

Little Ida Lewis Rk

Ida Lewis Rk

King Park

Brenton Cove

Historic shipwrecks are the property of the
State of Rhode Island, nothing may be removed.
Rhode Island Antiquities Act (G.L, Chp., 43.45.1)

Please read the "Preserving Shipwrecks" article
in this book.

Contributing Authors

Mark Bennett
PADI Certification 1987

Divemaster Certification 1989

Mark's diving experiences have been not only in the Newport/ Narragansett Bay area but also in Maine, New Hampshire, Arkansas, Florida's east coast and Keys, as well as in the Gulf of Mexico.

While in college, he operated a commercial diving business in Newport Harbor.

In the years 1987 through 1994, Mark was employed by a Rhode Island dive shop.

Spearfishing as well as artifact collecting are his primary diving interests.

Mark is a patrolman with the West Warwick Police Department.

Bob Cembrola
Bob grew up on the Warren waterfront. He has been diving since 1972 and has over 2,000 hours underwater.

Bob has worked on British frigates of 1778 in Narragansett Bay; the sunken city of Port Royal, Jamaica 1692; the pirate ship *Whydah* 1717; and the Lake George radeau of 1758, among others. He also consults as a marine archaeologist on a number of projects.

Bob was the Executive Director of the Marine Museum at Fall River, Massachusetts. He is currently curator of maritime history at the United States Naval War College in Newport, Rhode Island.

Steven Dumas
Steven has been an avid diver for the past 15 years. An insatiable desire to explore new sites and wrecks has led him to dive the Atlantic and Pacific coasts, the Hawaiian Islands, as well as the Gulf of Mexico.

He has worked as a commercial diver in the New England area on many projects and operations such as the Newport and Jamestown bridges.

Since he is an enthusiastic wreck diver, he enjoys visiting the many wrecks of Narragansett Bay and Rhode Island Sound.

A PADI Divemaster and the owner of the diving vessel *Alicia Marie*, Steven often runs charters to the *U-853* and other wrecks, sharing his knowledge and excitement of the ocean with fellow divers.

George Flynn
George Flynn attended The New York Phoenix Institute, The Pratt Art Institute, and The Pan American Art Institute. After

working for some of the most prestigious scholastic jewelers in the United States, George is now a free lance graphic designer and consultant. He lives with his family and Irish Wolfhound in Warwick, Rhode Island.

His love of diving began nearly twenty years ago. In addition to diving in Rhode Island waters, George has explored the ocean off California, Florida, and the exotic waters of the Caribbean.

Kenneth Fortier
PADI OWSI #27801

Certification Level: PADI Open Water Scuba Instructor

Dive Experience: First certified in 1981, Ken has assisted in PADI, NAUI, and YMCA scuba courses and currently teaches PADI Open Water, Advanced Open Water, Rescue Diver, and Divemaster courses.

Ken's diving experience includes: the coastal waters of Rhode Island, Connecticut, Massachusetts, Maine, New York, New Jersey, California, Florida, the Bahamas and Curacao; various inland waters of New England and New York; and dives of WW I, WW II and various other vessels. Ken worked as a research diver on 1991 and 1992 archeological projects of a French and Indian War vessel in Lake George,

New York and is an experienced Ice Diver.

He is the recipient of the Hometown Award, Waterbury, Connecticut, for rescuing a diver in Rhode Island waters.

Ken is an Assistant Vice President for a Connecticut bank, and is a Certified Information Systems Auditor.

Robert Frederiksen
A reporter at the Providence, Rhode Island *Journal-Bulletin*, Bob is a water rat, who has a life-long fascination with the sea and seafaring, sparked by co-ownership of a 30-foot-long ketch named *Dove*.

A native New Yorker, he attended city schools, served nearly four years in the Army Air Corps, later the Army Air Force, as an aerial engineer and crew chief on B-25 medium bombers, half that time in China, Burma, and India.

He graduated from Columbia College in 1950 and Columbia School of Journalism in 1951, then joined the Journal-Bulletin specializing in environmental reporting after stints as a city hall reporter and rewrite man.

Father of three children, all grown and flown to Houston, San Francisco, and Juneau, Alaska, he lives in Providence with a black cat named "Sasha".

Contributing Authors

William Gordon, Jr.

William R. Gordon, Jr. is an Assistant Professor in the Department of Marine Affairs at the University of Rhode Island.

Prior to arriving at URI in 1991, Dr. Gordon was an assistant professor of environmental planning at Southwest Texas State University in San Marcos, Texas. His specializations include artificial reef planning and management, as well as environmental planning and legal applications in coastal and marine settings.

He has served as an environmental consultant in various private, state and federal capacities. Recent projects in Rhode Island include developing the planning, guidance and permit requirements for the Rhode Island Department of Transportation in the demolition and deployment of the old Jamestown Bridge as a series of artificial reefs.

Professor Gordon has also been actively involved in designing comprehensive planning guidelines for the Atlantic States Marine Fisheries Commission for artificial reef planning activities along the entire East Coast and he has served as a federal reviewer on the Boston Harbor Tunnel Project.

Albert Langner

PADI Open Water 1981

PADI Advanced Open Water 1982, 569 career dives, 250 wreck dives

Most of Al's diving has been in Massachusetts and Rhode Island but he has been all up and down the east coast from New York to Maine. He has visited most of the known shipwrecks of New England and also has enjoyed the warm clear waters of Hawaii, Florida, and the Caribbean.

Preserving shipwreck artifacts has become a rewarding off season hobby.

He is employed by Connecticut General Life Insurance Company, Bloomfield, Connecticut.

Captain Bruce Mackin

NAUI 8925L

Bruce is a Coast Guard licensed Captain who began diving in 1962, was certified as a Divemaster in 1976, and became a NAUI Instructor in 1986.

He was awarded NAUI's Outstanding Service Award in 1992 for writing two NAUI specialty programs: The Uniformed Scuba Unit Search & Recovery program and the Advanced Search, Excavation & Recovery program.

Professionally, Bruce served 20 years as a fulltime Marine Police Officer and was the Police Diving Supervisor for 19 years. An avid wreck diver, he has been the first diver to explore numerous shipwrecks, including two Connecticut tugboats, the Condor and the Celtic.

Bruce dove in South Vietnam, the Caribbean, and several East Coast states from Massachusetts to Florida.

His artifacts have been featured on Cable Television in addition to being displayed in area museums, parks, and restaurants.

John Stanford

A Financial Analyst by profession, he has had a love of the sea and maritime history since early childhood. A certified diver since 1981, a PADI Rescue Diver and avid underwater photographer, his dive experiences have taken him to local waters, the U.S. Virgin Islands, the Bahamas and Mexico.

As owner and skipper of the diveboat *Endeavor II*, he, his wife, Karen, son, Sean, and small groups can be found anchored over one of the many

spots in this book on any given weekend during the dive season. His work has also appeared in *The Fisherman*. He is a resident of Warwick, Rhode Island.

Wayne Tripp

Wayne Tripp lives in Rhode Island with his wife, Robin, and their children, Heather and Dirk, a dog, two cats, and almost enough tropical marine fish.

An illustrator and jewelry designer by profession, he is an avid scuba diver, painter of miniature military figures, and marine fish-keeper.

A near legendary bug-hunter, he's decided to give the lobster population a chance to recover and devote all of his bottom time to observing and collecting marine tropicals. The lobsters love the idea.

Wayne's daughter, Heather, and son, Dirk, are following in their father's flipper steps. They accompany him at every opportunity, particularly on his tropical fish collecting expeditions.

Earth, Moon, Sun = Tides & Currents

by David Shelley

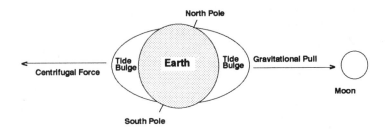

Tides Defined

Tides originate in the open ocean. *Tide* is the rise and fall of the ocean levels. *High Tide* occurs when *flood* water comes in from the ocean. Conversely, *low tide* or *ebb tide* occurs when that same water returns, ebbs, to the open ocean. *Tidal range*, a verticle measurement, is the difference between high and low tide—approximately 4 feet along the Rhode Island coastline.

Rhode Island has two high tides and two low tides every 24 hours. Approximately 12 1/2 hours pass between each high and low tide. It is about 6 1/4 hours from the beginning to the end of high tide.

Current is a horizontal motion of water from any cause. *Tidal current* is water flowing from high and low tides.

Earth, Moon, Sun

The earth revolves in an orbit around the sun, held there by the sun's gravity. Although the moon appears to orbit the earth, the two actually revolve around a common point, held in balance by their mutual gravitational attraction.

Tides are caused primarily by the gravitational force between the Earth and the moon, modified somewhat by the sun.

The moon pulls hardest on the side of Earth closest to it—as a result, the ocean bulges toward the moon.

The moon's pull is less on the opposite side of the Earth allowing centrifugal force to bulge the ocean away from the Earth.

The bulges stay in the same

relative positions as the Earth rotates underneath them causing the tide to *follow the moon.*

Spring Tides = Strong Currents
Greater than average tidal ranges (about 20%), called *spring tides,* occur and currents are significantly stronger during the month when the sun-moon-earth and the sun-earth-moon line up at new moon and at full moon respectively.

Know The Exceptions
The average swimming capability of scuba equipped divers is about one mile per hour. Most of the tidal currents in the prime dive spots are less than that.

However, location, water depth, phase of the moon, wave action, wind, and the like cause exceptions.

Some General Considerations
Tides higher than the 4 foot average cause stronger currents. Tides lower than the average result in less current.

Peak water flow occurs midway, approximately 3 hours, into the tide. The velocity of flow corresponds to this flow rate.

Slack tide for most of the bay is close to the end of high or low tide.

High tide generally produces better visibility. However, increased water flow can create turbulent conditions which may decrease visibility.

Study Your Chart
Study your Narragansett Bay chart. Observe where the water bottlenecks or funnels at flood and ebb tides. Consider the deep East Passage and the shallow West Passage.

Look at the passages and the topography of the various points of land and reefs, both above and below the water. Imagine how the water swirls around these obstacles while it floods and ebbs.

Do Your Homework
Before you leave to play on the bay check and see what the tide is doing.

Consult your tide tables, charts, calendars, the local newspaper, and listen to the weather report on radio or television.

NOAA publishes a booklet every year that covers tidal information for the continental USA.

There is some pretty slick computer software that will do everything except dive.

Fish Tales

by Wayne Tripp

Wolffish

A Bloated Face

I was diving for lobsters just outside of Fort Wetherill's West Cove, on the small island face that drops away to sixty feet. As I moved up the face of the cliff a large ominous black hole in the rock came into view.

Hovering a mere six inches from the opening, I held myself steady by gripping the edges of the hole with my hands and peered into the darkness. I was frozen with fear!

A bloated, Zombie grey face with an ugly gaping mouth brimming with crooked razor sharp fangs stared menacingly at me out of the darkness! The nightmare inches from my face and hands was a vicious 5-foot-long wolffish. Wolffish are so degenerate that they attack objects and humans without warning or provocation. Nearly swallowing my regulator, I backpedaled away from the cavern as fast as I could. The image of that nightmarish face haunts me to this day.

One Day At Point Judith...

To conserve air, George Flynn and I were snorkeling out to scuba dive at the tip of the east breakwater.

I was eager to get to the tip and do some serious lobster stalking.

Suddenly five or six black and white striped pilot fish swam by. I recalled that these little fish often accompanied sharks, hoping to share morsels from their dinner.

And sure enough, the sunlit water suddenly darkened as a huge gray head started to pass me on the left. My heart choked my throat—was this to be my first and last encounter with a shark? But just as suddenly, the head ended, and I saw the long top and bottom fins that terminated this ocean oddity. My "shark" was a gigantic but harmless ocean sunfish!

Wolves Of The Sea

I was midway through an afternoon lobster dive outside the West Cove at Fort Wetherill when I noticed that the bottom was covered with dead and dying silversides.

I immediately became engulfed in a school of these tiny striped fish and their killers—huge bluefish on a feeding frenzy!

During past fish massacres, I had witnessed at a distance the violence and carnage wrought by these wolves of the sea.

Instinctively I curled my fingers into my palms to keep them from being bitten off. Trembling with fear, I attempted to move away from the murderous activity that surrounded me.

I was being continually bumped as if the wolves were sizing me up for an attack. I made every effort to keep my wits about me as I moved slowly through the slaughter.

But as calmly and carefully as I inched away from the frenzied feeders, I became aware with rising panic that I wasn't leaving them behind. At first I thought they were following me, but careful observation—we were eyeball to eyeball—let me know that as I left some behind they were being quickly replaced by other larger, more deadly looking members of the *pack*. For ten of the longest minutes of my life—minutes which aged me years— I inched my way through the slaughterhouse.

The wolves continued to smash into me with ever increasing ferocity as I left the bay and swam through the rocky cut into Fort Wetherill's West Cove. The pack surrounded me until I was well into the cove. Gradually they thinned out— and then they were gone as if it had been nothing but a nightmare.

Guest Or Main Course?

It was over. Whether I was ever in any real danger or not, I don't know. But I'll never forget the day I found myself the unwilling guest—or was I nearly the main course?— at a bluefish banquet. I remember every time I go into the water.

89

Fish You Will Come To Know & Love

by Wayne Tripp

Your Buddies The Fish

One of the first marine creatures that new divers see is a fish. Knowing how to find and identify a few of Rhode Island's more common fishes increases the pleasure and thrill of diving

Cunner AKA Choggies

The most common fish, the cunner, or choggie, as it is locally called, is in the wrasse family. It's a small fish, 6 or 7 inches, varying in color from rusty brown to blue or greenish brown, with a typical fish shape. It is found in large groups, usually from mid-water to the bottom.

Tautog AKA Blackfish

Tautog or blackfish are also wrasses reaching about two feet in length. They are charcoal gray to black with a whitish throat and lips. Not the brightest of fish and sluggish, they're fairly easy to spear and make excellent eating.

Striped Bass

The striped bass is a much sought-after game fish, commonly 3 1/2 feet, easily recognized by its long silvery body decorated with dark horizontal pin-striping. Since the striper swims up rivers to spawn, it has suffered from pollution.

Eels

If you night dive or stick your head in holes looking for lobster, you may come face to face with conger eels.

Congers are long black snake-like fish that, like their cousins the moray eels, always seem to

have their mouths open menacingly. They mean you no harm;
this is just the way they breathe.
Don't touch the eels and they
won't touch you!

Flounder
Let's move along the bottom for
a moment and meet our next
two creatures. The flounder and
the barndoor skate are almost
always seen on the bottom resting flat, buried to their eyeballs
in sand.

Many a new diver has jerked
into a nervous back-flip when a
blossoming cloud of sand suddenly exploded upward. It
leaves the diver gasping,
"WHAT was THAT?" Just
a flounder,
that's all.

Bluefish
Even Rhode
Islanders who have
never slipped beneath the
waves can be aware of bluefish.
Most people who spend any
time around Narragansett Bay
have seen the surface of the
sea exploding with the frenzy of
feeding bluefish.

Blues are good-sized, up to four
feet in length, nasty-tempered,
silver-blue school-fish with
mouths crammed full of needle-
sharp teeth. Many a menhaden
has lost its life in the snapping
jaws of a hungry blue.

Sharks
Almost everyone who dives is
asked, time after time, if they've
ever been attacked by or at
least seen a shark.

In 20 years I've never seen a
shark while I was diving. No human has ever been attacked by
a shark in Narragansett Bay.

There are sharks of all sizes,
colors, and varieties: bull
sharks, blue sharks, and white
sharks to name a few but you
may never see one close to
shore.

In fact, a fellow diver and men-
tor, Bill Campbell, told a lecture
group that when looking
for blue sharks to film,
he had to go far off
the shores of Block
Island to find any.

Get A Fish Book
Although they're far
too numerous to describe
here, there are many other fish
in Rhode Island waters. A good
western Atlantic fish book will
enable the diver to identify most
of the creatures she or he will
encounter.

Whether you see large pollack
or tiny silversides, sea robins or
silvery scup, always remember
to keep looking. There's always
one you've never seen before.

Ice Diving—Exciting And Mystical

by **Kenneth R. Fortier**

With appreciation to:
  Don Maryland
  Bill Thomas
  Brian Wilcox

Ice Diving Is Worth It

For a few hardy souls, the danger, excitement, visual beauty, tranquility and mystical experience of ice diving makes all of the preparation worth-while.

Equipment and Procedures

Ice diving requires a dry suit and extensive practice in a swimming pool prior to the outdoor experience.

Select a mild day, dress in layers of warm clothing and wear a hat with ear protection.

Lines and Harnesses

A jacket-style chest harness is used under the buoyancy compensator. D-ring secured chest harnesses must also be secured with a weight-type belt buckle. The weight belt must be free to be dropped if required.

A safety line must be established for **each** diver—**no** shared lines! Use a floating 3/8 inch rope in excellent condition. Secure two loops at the end of the rope approximately two feet apart. To each loop attach a carabiner, at least one of which is a locking type. The carabiner will be secured directly to the diver's chest harness. Securely fasten the free end of the safety rope to an ice screw or ladder which cannot be dragged into the triangular opening in the ice.

Line Tenders

Assign an experienced line tender to each diver to keep his/her safety lines taut and tangle free. Determine all line signals before the dive.

Scuba Equipment

Exhaling into your regulator above water or placing it on the snow or ice can cause it to freeze-up and free flow. Use hot water to thaw frozen regulators.

Attach a 30 CF pony bottle to your scuba tank as a redundant air supply. Take a dive light.

Safety Diver
A fully suited safety diver, harnessed with a safety line that is at least fifty percent longer than the safety lines of the divers under the ice, must be standing by. If one of the divers under the ice becomes detached from the safety line, he/she immediately ascends to the under surface of the ice and hangs there vertically. The safety diver enters the opening and swims just under the surface of the ice to the end of her/his safety line. Keeping the line fully extended, the safety diver performs a 360 degree rotation under the ice until the safety line connects with the lost diver.

Safety Above All Else
Abort the dive under the following conditions: thin ice, running water, springs, recently formed or melting ice. For convenience and to reduce response time in emergency situations, select a spot near shore and your vehicle.

Water Depth Considerations
Deep water requires additional safety line and reduces bottom mobility. Shallow water reduces the depth under the ice.

Cutting the Opening
A triangular opening is not hard to cut and allows divers to exit the opening at the corners easily. The opening should be large enough to fit three divers.

Cutting must be performed by individuals in dry suits: (1) Using ice augers or choppers, drill a hole at each corner of the opening, (2) standing clear of the opening, use old fashioned ice saws to make straight cuts between the holes (unlike chain saws, ice saws are safe, make clean cuts, and leave no oil or gas in the water), (3) use ice choppers or shovels to push the ice plug under the ice. Move the plug far enough from the opening to stop it from sliding back into the opening. Keep safety lines clear of the plug.

Marking The Opening
After use, the opening must be clearly marked to avoid accidents. (1) To facilitate refreezing of the opening, replace the ice plug. (2) Chop shallow holes in the ice and encircle the opening with vertically placed branches which can be seen from a distance. (3) Place bright, biodegradable tape or cloth around the branches. When the opening is thoroughly refrozen, in several days, return and remove all of the litter.

Kayak Diving

by Dave Shelley

No Crowd Here

As I looked out of the car window, it became apparent that the dive site was at least a mile from shore. A quick check of the chart verified this observation.

The advice from the folks at the store was "You want lobster tonight, then go to this reef," so I decided I was hungry. It was lunacy to swim with full scuba gear for over a mile but easy to figure my next move. Out came the trusty kayak—well maybe off the roof of the car.

Yachting Anyone?

Kayak diving presents so many answers and so many opportunities one wonders, "Why isn't everyone kayaking?" Elusive as the answer to that query may be, I offer the following observation: the boat itself. When the vision of a kayak comes into focus most see a tipsy, sit-inside vessel requiring Eskimo-like heritage to keep upright. Not an incorrect picture for some kayaks.

For this story I have another personal yacht in mind. They're called sit-on-top kayaks. As the description implies—you sit on top, not inside.

The so called worst case scenario for this scuba diver/paddler on these PDC (personal diving craft) is that you might fall in the water.

Should this not be the time to execute your deep water entry, you simply right the kayak, if necessary, then climb back in. No rolls need be learned and nothing is lost or flooded since it was either down below or attached to the deck.

How About a Date?

Diving from a kayak offers freedom and versatility not easily matched by any one vessel. So if you are an average individual looking to have some above average fun, please, come and enjoy.

Now before you go off to join those kayakers and kayak divers who eagerly await you, consider this one tidbit of advice: get some education on kayak diving.

Diving and kayaking are like boy and girl. If only all marriages could be so much fun. But boy and girl don't always get along until they get to know each other.

Some stores and instructors offer formal training. This instruction is invaluable. (For you who question this advice perhaps you can help me out here and recall just how it was you got certified to scuba dive.)

Up/Down Fun!

With kayak and education in hand just what can you do now? Start with excursions described in the original *Rhode Island Adventure Diving* book or in this edition: *Rhode Island Adventure Diving II.*

For an exciting expedition, how about Gooseberry Island via Green Bridge? Couple the paddle of less than a mile with easy anchoring in the shallow water near the arches and you can't lose.

A similar dive would be Kettle Bottom Rock less than a mile from Fort Wetherill. Another possibility would be a "drift" dive along Beavertail. Towing the boat with you is no different than floating an inner tube, and don't you need to display your dive flag anyway? Sure beats swimming back to the boat or flailing those rocks in the surf with your body.

Speaking of surf, few thrills can match catching a wave when the weather makes diving a questionable activity. Again, because of the inherent safety sit-on-top kayaks offer, surfing is now another adventure instead of a sign of certain madness.

Adventure Awaits

So quit wondering and start doing! Beg, borrow, rent or buy a sit-on-top kayak today and start experiencing the adventure as well as reading about it.

For any of you doubting the benefits of these marvelous water craft, let me depart by telling you that the folks at the dive shop were right. After I was rewarded with a great dive that few shore sites could offer, I ate like a king!

Bug Hunting

by Wayne Tripp

American Lobster

(*Homarus americanus*)

- Five pairs of walking legs
- Can not swim
- Large muscular tail used for backward propulsion
- One pair of crusher, gripper claws
- Six pair of swimmerets
- Compound eyes on movable stalks can detect movement, may see
- Detachable legs & claws "autotomy" Self-amputated limbs regenerate
- Grow by molting "shedding"

Bug Hunting

Usually one of the first questions northern divers are asked as they come cold and dripping from the brine is "Did you catch anything?"

Most New Englanders asked to name the edible creatures inhabiting our waters would place Homerus Americanus somewhere near the top of their list. "What's that?" you ask.

Here are a few hints. Nowhere other than eastern North America are there any exactly like ours. Our Pilgrim forefathers once claimed anyone could walk along the shores and pick up ten or twelve pounders easily. As a food, it was considered cheap fare, fit only for the poor. Yes, it's the great American Bug...the Lobster.

Rules And Regulations

You must be a Rhode Island resident and have a Rhode Island lobster license to take any bugs. If you aren't sure you'll like lobstering enough to spend the money for a license, dive with a buddy who has a license. That buddy must be the one exiting the waters with the lobsters.

Legal lobsters must measure 3 1/4" from the rear of the eye socket to the rear of the carapace. Egg bearing females and undersized lobsters must be released immediately. You may hunt your lobsters day or night, but you may only take 8 lobsters in any twenty-four hour period.

Taking undersized lobsters and stealing from lobster pots is akin to horse stealing. Caught by the

Rhode Island Department of Environmental Management, the criminal's boat and diving equipment may be confiscated and she/he will go to court and be heavily fined. Caught by a lobsterman—you can imagine the consequences!

Once you catch a likely keeper, look underneath its tail. If you see dark berry-like eggs, it's a pregnant female.

Gently let her go. As you look at the tail, if there are no eggs, notice the first pair of swimmerets. If they are hard and grooved, it's a male. If they are soft and feathery, it is a female.

Day And Night Lobstering

The main difference between day and night lobstering, is that lobsters in the day time hole up in burrows, at night, the same lobsters are walking about.

To catch lobsters, divers may only use their hands. Nets, snares, hooks, spears, etc. are illegal.

Daytime lobstering is much more exciting and challenging because the lobster is backing further into its hole and fending off the diver by grabbing fingers and trying to crush them.

At night the diver sneaks up on the unsuspecting strolling bug, remembering that it can flit away to safety quite easily by jetting backwards. Care must be taken though. It is amazing how fast a hunted lobster can whip around and face a predator with two nasty bone-crushing claws.

Lobster claws can exert tremendous pressure, and it could hurt a lot. The best way to begin bug-hunting is probably to team up with a more experienced diver who's done it before.

Preparing Lobster

Assuming you've caught your lobsters, double checked their size, and brought them home in an ice-filled cooler, it is time to cook them.

There are many methods and recipes: for many people, the simpler the better. Plunge live lobsters head first into a pot of boiling water. Cook an average sized lobster for twelve minutes—more pounds, more time.

Eating Lobster

You'll need a pair of nutcrackers and picks to get at your feast. You may eat meat from both claws, the tail, and upper legs if you don't mind a little work.

Some people also eat the red coral or roe, and the green tomalie. The coral tastes a bit like cheese—cats love it. Once cooked, add a little drawn butter and dig in.

Phantom Ship

by Marlene & Don Snyder

The Palatine's Flaming Image

Before there were UFOs, there were monsters of the deep and phantom ships condemned to sail the seas for eternity.

Both the *Flying Dutchman* and the *Palatine* were legendary doomed ships.

Nearly 300 years after her disappearance, if she ever really existed, the flaming specter of the *Palatine* continues to haunt the shores of Block Island and the minds of those who visualize her incendiary image.

The Phantom Ship

All we know for sure is that sometime in the early 1700s a ship, perhaps the *Palatine,* with 364 European immigrants aboard, enroute to Philadelphia, foundered, burned, and vanished (for a time) off Sandy Point's Cow Cove, Block Island.

Tall Kattern, The Witch

Little is known of the three survivors of the *Palatine*, that is, except for Tall Kattern.

As legend has it, Tall Kattern was a statuesque young woman "reputedly endowed with occult faculties." She was "gifted with second sight and other weird phenomena." Kattern also had frequent trance-like episodes.

Labeled a witch by the Islanders who feared her, Tall Kattern's post trance remembrances created much of the mystery and legend surrounding the *Palatine*.

Lured Ashore?

It is doubtful, as some including the poet John Greenleaf Whittier have said, that the *Palatine* was lured ashore on the night after Christmas 1738 by Block Island wreckers, who then murdered the passengers and crew, plundered the ship, set her on fire, and cast her adrift.

Others have speculated that the captain and crew died with their passengers after having intentionally grounded and torched the ship off Block Island in an ill conceived plan to rob and abandon the immigrants.

Closer to the truth, perhaps, is an article that appeared in the September 8, 1947 *Providence Journal* :

"The burial ground on Block Island of 20 Dutch immigrants yesterday received its first marker, a monument of native granite, 209 years after their *Palatine* ship was wrecked off Old Cow's Cove. . . .Islanders rescued 100 passengers and crew members. . . Eighty survived to continue their journey but the other 20 died and were buried on the Island."

The dedication and placement of a monument by the Block Islanders over a group of mounds, said to be the graves of the passengers, was meant to set the record straight—but did it?

So He Sent Fire
Up until the late 1800s, the *Palatine* reportedly reappeared off Sandy Point, Block Island, in full flame, to countless "reliable" witnesses on the anniversary of its disappearance.

In 1869, John Congdon, a 92 year-old resident of South County, who claimed to have seen the flaming ship "eight or ten times", wrote: "so He (God) sent the Fire or Phantom Ship to let them (the Block Islanders) know He had not forgotten their wickedness. She was seen once a year, on the same night of the year on which the murder occurred, so long as any of the wreckers were living, but never after all were dead." In 1905 the Newport *Mercury* reported that "Scores of reputable men . . (have sailed close enough to see the apparition) . . .masts, sails and ropes . . . and even persons in the flaming rigging."

The Dancing Mortars
Beams of lignum vitae salvaged from the *Palatine* were made into mortars for grinding meal.

It was reported, originally by an "inveterate opium-eater", that on the date of the tragedy each year the mortars "would fall over on their sides, roll back and forth across the floor, right themselves and then dance up and down (often) so high that they touched the ceiling."

"It's A Spirit Ship"
Quoted in the *Providence Sunday Journal Magazine*, August 4, 1985, diver and author Jim Jenney said: "Nobody's ever found it. It's a spirit ship."

Preserving Rhode Island's Underwater Shipwrecks

Rhode Island
Historical Preservation & Heritage Commission
150 Benefit Street, Providence, Rhode Island 02903
401-277-2678 • FAX 401-277-2968 • TDD 401-277-3700

Our Maritime Heritage

Historic shipwrecks on the bottom of Narragansett Bay are part of the maritime heritage of the Ocean State. Resting beneath Rhode Island waters are colonial trading ships, war ships from the American Revolution, and steamers from the nineteenth century. Historic shipwrecks, like historic sites on land, can contribute much to our understanding of history. They are important to all of us because they help explain the heritage that makes us Rhode Islanders.

Rhode Island Antiquities Act

The Rhode Island Antiquities Act (Chapter 43.45.1 of the General Laws) states that historic shipwrecks and the artifacts they contain are state property. Narragansett Bay belongs to all the people of Rhode Island, and state government is responsible for regulating such things as fishing, water pollution, access, and shipwrecks to protect the public's rights.

State Underwater Archaeology Program

Rhode Island's underwater archaeology program is administered by the Rhode Island Historical Preservation & Heritage Commission (RIHPHC), the state office for historical preservation. The RIHPHC maintains files on the locations of historic shipwrecks and issues permits for their study.

Archaeological study is conducted under strict controls. Detailed records are kept allowing reconstruction of the site on paper in the laboratory. With proper study, a full story of the ship, its crew, and its cargo is revealed and preserved. Artifacts recovered without following the proper methods for recovery and study are meaningless, and when not handled carefully with modern conservation techniques, they disintegrate and are lost forever.

Preserving Shipwrecks

Most divers understand the importance of leaving shipwrecks undisturbed so other divers can explore them and so that marine archaeologists can study them. But a few irresponsible divers regard wreck sites as private finds, and they loot these sites for personal pleasure or private gain. Whether a diver takes a few "souvenirs" for a personal collection or a diver strips an entire shipwreck and sells the artifacts for profit, he or she is stealing from the rest of us, and he or she is breaking the law.

If you know the location of a shipwreck contact the RIHPHC. The information that you provide will be added to their inventory and will help in planning for the scholarly and recreational use of the state's historic shipwrecks. Please do not remove any artifacts. A number of sport divers are working with the RIHPHC already by sharing information about the wrecks they have found and explored. The RIHPHC needs and welcomes this help.

Responsible Sport Divers

Sport divers who explore wrecks and who follow the preservation ethic are partners of the RIHPHC and the best source of new information.

These divers help assure that Rhode Island's historic shipwrecks remain undisturbed so our children and grandchildren will have the same opportunity that we have to study and enjoy this important part of our our common heritage.

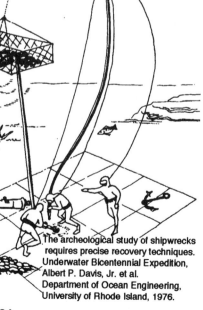

The archeological study of shipwrecks requires precise recovery techniques. Underwater Bicentennial Expedition, Albert P. Davis, Jr. et al. Department of Ocean Engineering, University of Rhode Island, 1976.

The Seals of Narragansett Bay

by **Steven Dumas**

Our Friends The Seals

For several months of the year, a special treat is in store for the observant Rhode Island boater. As the water turns cold in late October, our playful friends, the seals, begin to arrive in Narragansett Bay.

Harbor Seals

The Harbor seal (*Phoca vitulina*) is by far the most common seal found wintering in Narragansett Bay. Weighing up to 300 pounds and not usually more than 6 feet in length, the Harbor seal is the smallest of the seals to visit our coast. Harbor seals vary in color, but are usually off gray with black or brown spots.

Gray Seals

Gray seals (*Halichoerus grypus*) are also very common along our coast. Slightly larger than the Harbor seal, Gray seal males can weigh up to 800 pounds with a length of up to 12 feet. Off shore rocks and islands are the preferred habitat of the Gray seal.

Seal Encounters

Some of the first seal encounters of the year are often reported by the local commercial fishing community. Fishermen speak of seals following their vessels for hours, sometimes as a playful gesture, but more often to steal the fish from a freshly baited lobster trap.

During the winter months, many fishermen avoid placing their fishing gear in areas frequented by seals. It seems that the seals are so efficient at removing the bait fish from the traps, that efforts to fish in these areas are wasted.

Spy Hopping The Intruder

At times, seals can be very curious animals. When a boater encounters a seal by chance, the seal will usually investigate the strange human visitor from a safe distance.

The author perceives this behavior as similar to the whale's "spy hopping". The seal will pop up in several different locations around the boat, trying to improve his vantage point of the intruder. If the observer is careful not to approach or disturb the seals, they may remain in the area for extended periods of time.

Seal Ledge

Sport fishermen and divers who navigate the waters of Brenton reef often encounter seals during the winter months. The abundance of fish and the outcroppings of rocks that form the reef make a perfect habitat for the marine mammals.

One such location on the reef has been named Seal Ledge because of their abundance throughout the winter. Boaters passing the ledge in winter will usually encounter the seals, either sun bathing on the rocks or swimming in the shallow waters that surround the ledge. Many skin and scuba divers who visit the reef to harvest fish interact with them.

Be aware that the seals may be near by at any time. It is essential that divers be conscious of their actions to avoid bringing harm to them.

Never seek out seal encounters but rather understand and co-exist in a way that is least interactive with them.

Protect Our Seal Friends

The Narragansett Bay seal population is protected by law; any harassment of seals could lead to a $10,000 fine and a 2 year prison term.

Because of their playful nature and curiosity, many seals are injured and killed every year by indirect human contact.

A seal may easily become entangled in a local fisherman's gill net and drown, or perhaps strangle or suffocate from the litter tossed from a visiting cruise ship. If everyone takes responsibility for their actions, a safe future will be assured for our winter guests.

Invaders Hit Coastal Waters

by Wayne Tripp

Bicolor Damselfish

Foureye butterflyfish

Unwilling Travelers

In late summer and early fall each year tropical fish eggs and, occasionally, full grown tropical fish become unwilling travelers on warm core rings of water that break away from the Gulf Stream and swirl one hundred fifty miles to Rhode Island's coastal and bay waters.

Arriving Ahead Of Schedule

With each passing year the tropicals seem to be arriving ahead of schedule and, de-lightfully, in much greater numbers and variety.

Goatfish

It has been speculated that the greater numbers of tropical fish being hatched earlier each year in warm tidal pools may be attributable to a slight, almost imperceptible warming of Rhode Island coastal waters.

One Day At King's Beach

In one day at Kings's Beach in Newport, my daughter and I counted 25 young spotfin butterflyfish. Tiny bicolor damsels flitted everywhere; only the cunners, our local pests, were more numerous.

Winter Kill

On that same day I found a full grown butterfly fish hiding under a ledge thirty feet down.

Full grown tropical fish are rarerly seen in Rhode Island coastal waters because they are strong enough swimmers to remain with the Gulf Stream when the core rings break off and swirl to the coast.

104

The tropical fish that are hatched in late summer and late fall never grow to maturity because they are biologically unequipped for cold water and die as soon as the water turns cold.

Rare Trunkfish
One day in mid-July I was hunting lobsters in Fort Wetherill's West Cove.

I found a likely burrow with a promising pair of claws sticking out. Carefully stalking closer, I brushed some yellow-brown seaweed away from the mouth of the lobster hole. The seaweed was the common kind that has little roundish air bladders (bladder wrack or rockweed).

Beaugregory

To my surprise one of the bladders swam back against the current to the mouth of the hole. Curious now, I took a second closer look, and realized this half-inch seaweed bladder had little eyes.

Trunkfish

Slowly, I detected a mouth, fins and tail. I was looking at the juvenile form of a boxfish, or trunkfish. In twenty years of diving, I'd never seen one before.

Migration to Invasion
Throughout the summer and fall, we found tropicals on almost all of our dives. Spotfin butterflies, bicolor damsels, goatfish, jewel damsels, foureyed butterflies, and squirrelfish all finned by, ogling we bubblebreathers.

Ocean To Aquarium
On one dive in August, my daughter, Heather, found and caught a tiny quarter-inch flash of bright blue and yellow.

This fish turned out to be a beaugregory, a damselfish neither of us had ever seen in these waters. Now, in February, that beaugregory is still flitting about in Heather's tank. He's grown to be about 2 inches long and seems to thrive in captivity.

To Our Memories
Unfortunantly, none of the butterflyfish did as well.

Try as we might, they seemed to live a week or two, and then perish. Perhaps they are a fish best enjoyed during the dive and then kept in our memories.

A Reporter Remembers The *U-853*

by Robert C. Frederiksen

Summer Palace

It was a fine summer morning in 1960, and I was piloting the 38-foot cabin cruiser *Summer Palace* toward the wreck of the German submarine *U-853* seven miles east of Block Island and 130 feet down.

Ordinarily, I would have been pounding a typewriter at the *Providence Journal-Bulletin* where I was, and still am, a reporter. But, an editor had heard that the sub was to be raised and wanted a first-hand story.

Swashbuckling Scuba Diver

Burton H. Mason, a swashbuckling diver from Trumbull, Connecticut had said that he would raise the sub.

Local divers had visited the sub off and on, lured by reports of treasure aboard. Some had blown off a propeller and dis-

played it in Newport. But Mason said that the only treasure would be found in exhibiting the *U-853*, like a U-boat in Chicago that was drawing mobs.

Sub-Marine Associates

I boarded the *Summer Palace* early that morning in Newport. I then woke Mason and Davis Trisko, another diver of Sub-Marine Associates Inc., and helped get them underway.

They gave me the wheel and the course to Block Island and then went back to sleep. Such confidence, or was it their hangovers? I wondered.

As I edged away from the dock, I saw a line of Navy destroyers knifing up the East Passage of Narragansett Bay with signal flags snapping. I wondered if that's how it looked when the *U-853* and her crew of 55 were being depth charged to death May 6, 1945, the day after she torpedoed and sank the American collier *Black Point* off Point Judith, Rhode Island.

To Shoot Sharks
As soon as we anchored, Mason and Trisko donned their wet suits and tumbled overboard, leaving me with a .32-caliber revolver and directions to shoot any sharks that showed up.

They returned to the surface about 45 minutes later, excited over having been inside the sub and removing a crewman's inflatable escape device.

Fortunately for me no sharks appeared. The gun barrel was plugged. If I had fired, it probably would have exploded, and I'd be typing this one-handed.

Mason Kept Me Posted
I recall Mason showing me color movies he had taken inside the sub of skeletons, eels, and German war slogans scrawled on the torpedo tubes. He phoned me frequent progress reports, which I turned into stories.

Skeleton Removed
One was on the removal of the skeleton of a German sailor from the *U-853*. The skeleton was buried with full military honors in Newport, but led to strong demands by the German government and U.S. Navy that the remains of the other crewmen not be disturbed. They weren't, but I suspect it was because Mason had already decided to drop the project because of the mounting costs.

Hannes Keller
Mason had attracted the interest of a Swiss diver-mathematician named Hannes Keller who had worked out tables for mixing various gases and compressed air that would shorten the decompression time of divers.

Mason and Keller talked of plugging the holes in the sub, then pumping air into her to bring her up, but nothing came of it.

Salvage Company
A New York salvage company quietly looked into raising the *U-853* in 1968, but nothing came of that either.

Larchmont Souveniers
Mason later removed items from the wreck of the passenger side-wheeler *Larchmont* off Watch Hill to be made into lamps, ashtrays and the like for Bloomingdale's in New York.

He gave me an ashtray made out of a crumpled piece of a steam pipe from the *Larchmont's* boiler room. I misplaced it or gave it away, or something. Now, I wish that I still had it, just for the memories.

Wreck Finding
by Captain Bruce Mackin, Article and Graphics

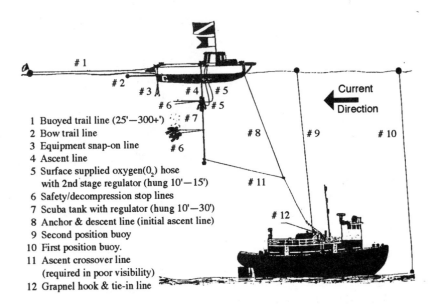

Current Direction

1 Buoyed trail line (25'—300+')
2 Bow trail line
3 Equipment snap-on line
4 Ascent line
5 Surface supplied oxygen(O_2) hose
 with 2nd stage regulator (hung 10'—15')
6 Safety/decompression stop lines
7 Scuba tank with regulator (hung 10'—30')
8 Anchor & descent line (initial ascent line)
9 Second position buoy
10 First position buoy.
11 Ascent crossover line
 (required in poor visibility)
12 Grapnel hook & tie-in line

The Search
At a minimum your electronic equipment should include a bottom recorder and a positioning device such as a Long Range Navigation system, (LORAN C) or a Global Positioning System (GPS).

The bottom recorder should be able to show a graphic readout of the ocean bottom and the wreck, either on a video screen or a paper print-out. The positioning device will enable you to determine where you are, and to record the wreck's position so that you can return to it in the future.

Most of the newer LORAN C and GPS units provide both Latitude/Longitude degrees, or LORAN, Line of Position (LOP) figures. To accurately record the wreck sites as they relate to each other and the surrounding area, a NOAA chart is necessary. If a LORAN C positioning device is used, the chart must be LORAN C overprinted.

Setting The Position Buoy
Once you think that you are close to the site, set the first anchored position buoy as a reference point for the surface search pattern.

Monitor your search pattern sweeps by using the buoy as a reference point.

The search pattern used and the distance between each sweep will depend on many factors, including the accuracy of your research, the size of the search area, the depth, the size of the wreck, and the quality of your electronics.

Monitor your bottom recorder to determine any abnormal bottom relief with a profile that would indicate the wreck.

Once located, record the location displayed on your positioning device and deploy the second anchored position buoy on the wreck.

Make a few additional sweeps around the buoy and over the wreck to confirm that something is below and that it was not a false reading.

Grapnel Hook

When you are satisfied that your positioning buoy is anchored in the wreck, take a few minutes to monitor your vessel's movement as it is affected by both the wind and current.

Move up wind/current of the second position buoy to a point that the bottom recorder indicated as the edge of the wreck. Lower a grapnel hook to the bottom, and after allowing additional line for scope, secure the line to your search vessel.

Allow the wind/current to push your vessel back over the wreck, or, if necessary, use your engine to back down in order to drag the grapnel hook up and into the wreck. Once you are hooked in, monitor your movement to be sure that you are not drifting off station.

This is easily accomplished by watching for any significant change in distance between your vessel and the position buoy that is in the wreck.

Divers Down

Once you have determined that you are not drifting, the first divers can descend.

The first diver down secures the grapnel hook into the wreck by using an independent line, chain, or cable. This prevents the hook from becoming dislodged from the wreck when there is a change of wind/current direction or sea conditions.

The dive leader will determine how and by whom the grapnel hook will be released at the end of the dive.

Wreck finding requires infinite time and patience. The satisfaction of finding a virgin wreck is worth the effort!

Researching for Shipwrecks

by Captain Bruce Mackin

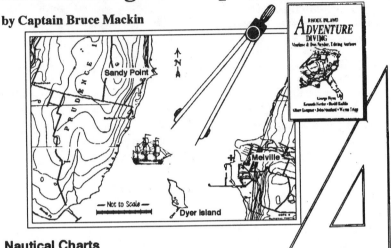

Nautical Charts

The chance of locating a shipwreck while diving without having conducted some previous research is slim.

On nautical charts, for example, a wreck may be recorded in several different ways. If an object on the bottom is known to be that of a wreck or wreckage, the site may be accurately labeled accordingly. But if a wreck or wreckage is additionally marked with the designation 'PA', it indicates that the position is approximate and not accurately recorded on the chart. In some cases, areas labeled 'obstruction' or 'rocks' have actually been found to be shipwrecks.

Older charts are worth researching too. Often, as the years pass and a wreck settles into the bottom, collapses, or is simply overlooked when the charts are being updated, the wreck's position may be omitted on the newer printings.

Sources Of Information

Sources such as U.S. Coast Guard reports and records, newspapers, microfilm reprints, historical materials, dive publications, and the numerous recent writings on shipwrecks and their locations will start you in the right direction.

In the larger cities, inquire if the libraries have the *Lloyd's Register,* the *Lloyds Weekly Shipping Index,* or the *Merchant Steam Vessels of the United States* for more detailed information. If you feel adventurous, head to Washington, D.C. and visit the National Archives, the Library of Congress, the Hydrographic

Survey Office, and the Smithsonian Institute. You will be amazed at the information available.

While conducting research pertaining to a particular location, keep note of the past names once associated with the various areas. It is not uncommon for the names of reefs, islands, and even land points to change over the years.

Personal Interviews

Personal interviews with long-time residents can often be quite rewarding. Not only can their stories be fascinating, but they may recall unrecorded nautical mishaps and their locations.

Talking with area fishermen, especially those who depend upon fishing for their livelihood, is an excellent source for determining shipwreck locations. You will probably find that most commercial fishermen are secretive about their productive fishing grounds. Therefore, before they give you their coordinates, you will have to convince them that you pose no threat to their productivity.

Never Give Up

Many frustrated divers could have avoided disappointment if they had only continued researching long enough to discover that the wreck that they thought they had discovered had actually been salvaged.

If the wreck was only partially salvaged or its cargo jettisoned, this information will be important when trying to verify the ship's identity once located. Any information relating to the size, construction, rigging, cargo, or propulsion is helpful for identification purposes.

Consult A Maritime Attorney

If your research reveals any information that the wreckage is lying in a state or a federally controlled preserve, you must check with the proper authority **prior** to any diving on the site.

Historic shipwrecks are the property of the State of Rhode Island, nothing may be removed. Rhode Island Antiquities Act (G.L, Chp., 43.45.1)

Please read the "Preserving Shipwrecks" article in this book.

If you intend to remove any artifacts or parts of the wreck, you must be absolutely sure that the wreck is abandoned and that there are no legal claims or restrictions.

If you discover anything during your research that suggests a legal complication, consult an experienced maritime attorney **prior** to any in-water activities related to the wreck.

Please protect our heritage.

Wreck Salvage Lift Bags

by Captain Bruce Mackin, Article & Graphics

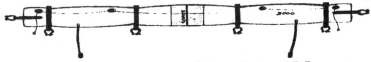

Ocean Salvage Tube—Salvage Pontoon Lift Bag

Bringing The Treasure Up

If the "treasures" that we find are too heavy to safely swim to the surface, how do we get them up?

The lift bag is the most common device used by recreational divers. There are three basic lift bag designs: salvage pontoons, pillow bags, and envelope bags.

Pontoon And Pillow Lift Bags

The smallest pontoon bag has a lifting capacity in excess of 1,000 pounds. The lifting capacity of the smallest pillow bags is 200 pounds. Both are built for commercial salvage operations. Towed along the surface, they are too large and bulky to be used by a recreational diver.

Envelope Lift Bags

The choice of most recreational divers is the envelope lift bag. Made in lifting capacities that range from less than 50 pounds to over 70,000 pounds, they are both simple and efficient. A bag with 100 pounds of lifting capacity, for example, can be rolled up and stored in a buoyancy compensator pocket or tool bag. Another advantage of the envelope lift bag is that it has an open bottom which allows for inflation without the need for special hoses or valves.

Envelope Lift Bag

Lift Bag Disadvantages

One disadvantage is the possibility of losing air out of the bottom as it is being towed along the surface.

Another disadvantage is that its lifting capacity must be closely matched to the weight of the object that is being recovered. If you use an envelope lift bag with a capacity far greater than the weight of the object being retrieved, a problem may result. As the bag and object ascend and the air volume in the bag increases (Boyle's Law), exces-

112

sive speed and force builds; upon reaching the surface, the lift bag may actually come out of the water.

If the lift bag comes out of the water it may fall to the side, deflate and sink back to the bottom. Not only does this increase your chance of losing the salvaged object and the lift bag, you also risk the safety of the divers below.

Inflating The Lift Bag
Use an independent source of air to inflate the lift bag.

Use of your regulator is **dangerous** for several reasons: it diminishes your life supporting air, it can cause a first stage freeze-up and regulator malfunction, and if your regulator's second stage becomes entangled in the lift bags rigging, you may be dragged to the surface by the ascending lift bag.

The proper method for inflating the envelope lift bag is to use short blasts of air from the independently supplied air gun.

Inflate the bag to the point that its effect on the object being salvaged is slightly positive. The lift bag, with its salvage in tow, will start to ascend to the surface gradually gaining speed as the air inside the bag expands.

Lift Bag Rigging
Lift bag rigging, whether chain, cable, rope, or a commercially made strap, should be capable of supporting at least three times the lift bag's capacity.

Attach A Line
Attach a line to the object being salvaged prior to lifting it. Snap the opposite end of the line around your descent line. If the descent line is too far from the object being salvaged, anchor the opposite end to the bottom.

Allow enough extra line to compensate for wind and current. This simple step will prevent your lift bag and object from drifting away once it arrives on the surface. If the lifting system fails, the line will make relocating your set-up easier.

Improvising A Lift Bag
A small lift bag can be improvised by placing a plastic garbage bag in a mesh catch bag and using the handles as a rigging point. Even an inverted five gallon bucket has worked.

ode to my poet forefathers

they sat as i beneath these stars
that they might etch
upon the scroll of life
a passing cloud
tinged with fire
perchance
a shooting star
to trace
upon the night
no falling tear
escapes
such faithful eye
save that truth
no quill may speak
they sat as i beneath these stars

By Mark Snyder
1991